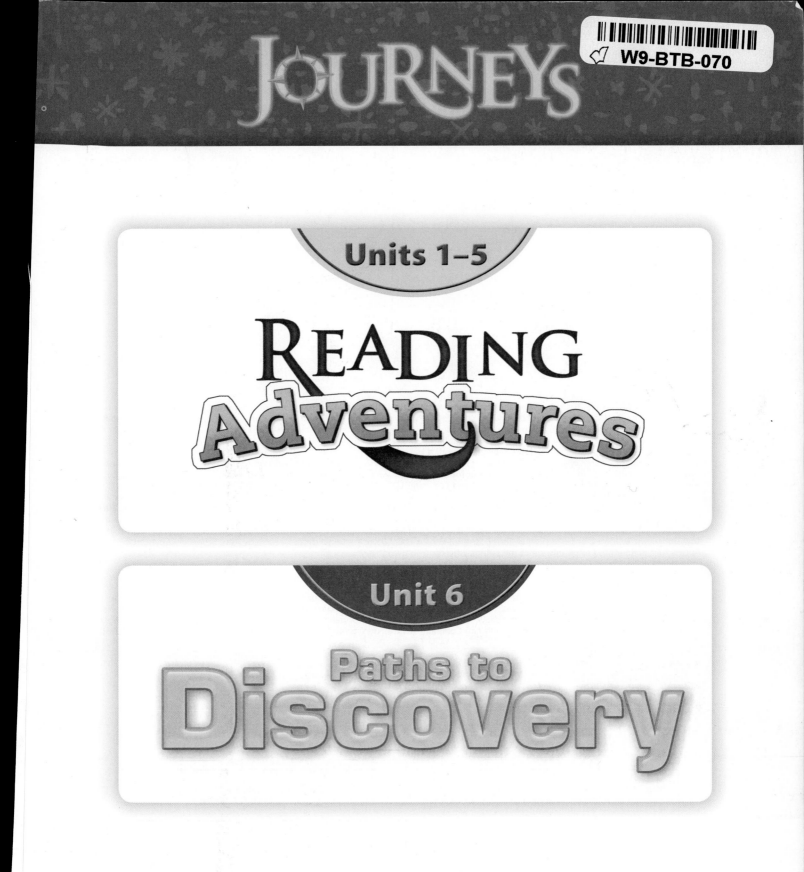

Journeys

Units 1–5

Reading Adventures

Unit 6

Paths to Discovery

HOUGHTON MIFFLIN HARCOURT
School Publishers

W9-BTB-070

From *The Panic Broadcast: Portrait of An Event* by Howard Koch. Copyright © 1970 by Howard Koch. Reprinted by permission of International Creative Management and the Estate of Howard Koch. From *Pyramids Around The World* by Orli Zuravicky. Copyright © 2004 by the Rosen Publishing Group, Inc. Reprinted by permission of the publisher. "Spider Ropes" from *A Nest Full of Stars* by James Berry. Text copyright © 2002 by James Berry. Reprinted by permission of HarperCollins Publishers. "The Spider" by Jack Prelutsky from *Something Big Has Been Here*. Copyright © 1990 by Jack Prelutsky. Reprinted by permission of HarperCollins Publishers. "The Poison-Dart Frogs" from *Lizards, Frogs, and Polliwogs* by Douglas Florian. Copyright © 2001 by Douglas Florian. Reprinted by permission of Houghton Mifflin Harcourt Publishing Company. "Toad by the Road" from *Toad by the Road: A Year in the Life of These Amazing Amphibians* by Joanne Ryder. Text copyright © 2007 by Joanne Ryder. Reprinted by permission of Henry Holt and Company, LLC. "Museum Farewell" by Rebecca Kai Dotlich. Text copyright © 2007 by Rebecca Kai Dotlich. Reprinted by permission of Curtis Brown Ltd. "The Comb of Trees" by Claudia Lewis from *Up In the Mountains: And Other Poems of Long Ago*. Text copyright © 1991 by Claudia Lewis. Reprinted by permission of HarperCollins Publishers. "Naming the Turtle" by Patricia Hubbell from *The Tigers Brought Pink Lemonade*. Text copyright © 1988 by Patricia Hubbell. Reprinted by permission of the author c/o Marian Reiner, Literary Agent. "Greater Flamingo" from *An Old Shell: Poems of the Galapagos* by Tony Johnston. Text copyright © 1999 by Tony Johnston. Reprinted by permission of Farrar, Straus & Giroux LLC. "Dinosaur Bone" from *Keepers* by Alice Schertle. Copyright © 1996 by Alice Schertle. Reprinted by permission of the author, who controls all rights.

Copyright © 2012 by Houghton Mifflin Harcourt Publishing Company

All rights reserved. No part of this work may be reproduced or transmitted in any form or by any means, electronic or mechanical, including photocopying or recording, or by any information storage and retrieval system, without the prior written permission of the copyright owner unless such copying is expressly permitted by federal copyright law. Requests for permission to make copies of any part of the work should be addressed to Houghton Mifflin Harcourt Publishing Company, Attn: Contracts, Copyrights, and Licensing, 9400 South Park Center Loop, Orlando, Florida 32819.

Printed in the U.S.A.

ISBN: 978-0-547-59579-5

7 8 9 10   0868   20 19 18 17 16 15 14 13 12

4500352737   B C D E F G

If you have received these materials as examination copies free of charge, Houghton Mifflin Harcourt Publishing Company retains title to the materials and they may not be resold. Resale of examination copies is strictly prohibited.

Possession of this publication in print format does not entitle users to convert this publication, or any portion of it, into electronic format.

READING Adventures

A Storm at Sea

by George Capaccio
illustrated by Craig Orback

Nathaniel Benjamin Moss lay on his bunk thinking about home. Maybe his mother was right. Maybe he never should have left Massachusetts to be a cabin boy on a whaling ship. It had been only three weeks since the *Amanda Pierce* had set sail from Gray's Wharf in New Bedford, but already Nathaniel wondered if he had made the right decision.

The worst part, Nathaniel thought, wasn't the food, although that was horrible. It wasn't even the way the rest of the crew treated him, calling him a "greenie" because he had never been to sea before. No, the worst part was how much he missed his family.

It didn't help, either, that the ship was always rolling. It rolled up and over the waves. It creaked and moaned. Feeling sick to his stomach, the boy forced himself to stand up. He still had to light the lamps on deck and then help Mr. Tombey, the cook, with supper. *Maybe it won't be so bad,* he thought, *once we get our first whale.*

Nathaniel went up on deck. A steady wind was gathering force. The sun had nearly set, and it was turning the ocean orange. Captain Brayshaw was taking his turn at the ship's wheel. Nathaniel liked the captain. He was a stern man from Boston, but he treated the men fairly. Nathaniel thought he was a fitting captain for one of the oldest whaling ships out of New Bedford.

After he lit the whale oil lamps along the sides of the ship, Nathaniel headed for the galley to help prepare supper. He could hear Mr. Tombey muttering, his accent getting stronger as he got madder. Mr. Tombey was from Barbados. Nathaniel knew Barbados was an island, but he knew nothing more about it—except that the ship wasn't sailing anywhere near Barbados on its way to the Indian Ocean. He didn't think Mr. Tombey was too happy about that. Nathaniel hoped the cook's longing for home would not make him impatient with Nathaniel himself.

In the galley, Nathaniel went to work dishing boiling-hot codfish soup into bowls for the captain and officers. He could feel Mr. Tombey's icy eyes on him. Nathaniel knew he had better not spill even a drop of soup. But the sea was getting rougher by the minute. Food was spilling all over the place.

Without warning, the galley door flew open. The first mate, a tall, heavyset man named Mr. Turner, ducked inside and slammed the door shut. Nathaniel dropped the ladle. Hot soup scalded his hand. Mr. Tombey glared at him. "Your job is to serve the food I make," the cook yelled, "not to waste it!"

"All hands on deck!" Mr. Turner shouted. "Even you, cabin boy. There's a gale blowing." The first mate grabbed Nathaniel's arm and led him toward the door.

Up on deck, Mr. Turner threw a jacket at Nathaniel. "You and Douglas have first watch tonight. It'll be cold up there. Call out if you see a whale or another ship."

Nathaniel made his way across the deck. A frosty wind blocked him at every step. The ship rocked in the mighty waves. Suddenly, what looked like a twenty-foot wave rolled over the left side of the deck and smashed into the boy's face. Nathaniel lost his balance and fell. He grabbed the nearest mast and held on for dear life. Nathaniel knew he might have been swept overboard if not for the securely anchored mast in the middle of the ship.

"Moss!" a voice roared. "Get on your feet! I need you up here!" Nathaniel raised his head. The main mast soared above him. Halfway up he saw, almost lost in the rigging, the unmistakable face of Mr. Douglas, the ship's blacksmith.

As Nathaniel began climbing the mast, Mr. Douglas yelled down. "If we don't get these sails furled in a hurry, the wind will rip them to shreds!" Nathaniel climbed faster, stepping carefully so that his feet wouldn't slip.

High above the deck, Nathaniel could feel every dip and rise the ship took in the storm. The wind shrieked as it blew across the ropes that held the sails. Nathaniel and Mr. Douglas scrambled up and across the rigging, working as hard and as fast as they could.

Nathaniel admired the blacksmith's strength and agility. Mr. Douglas was an old man, but his age didn't prevent him from climbing up the ropes and rolling up the main sail. The two worked without speaking as they moved smoothly in a kind of dance. After finishing the job together, they stood side by side.

When all the sails were furled, most of the sailors
went back below deck to settle in for the night. The ship's
bell struck eight times. The first watch had begun and
would last until midnight. To make sure the voyage was
successful, the crew took turns watching for whales around
the clock. Tonight was Nathaniel and Mr. Douglas's turn.
Side by side, they balanced on a large rope high above the
deck and leaned on a furled sail. The wind had died down,
but the sea still swelled and the ship rocked end to end.
Nathaniel held tight to the sail. He was glad he hadn't
eaten supper.

As he scanned the horizon for whales, Nathaniel thought
back to the clear, bright morning when the ship pulled out of
the dock at Gray's Wharf. He would never forget the date—
March 3, 1834—and the excitement of his leaving. He closed
his eyes for a moment.

With a jolt, Nathaniel felt Mr. Douglas's weighty hand on his shoulder. "Keep your eyes open, Moss! You're standing watch now. Don't be drifting off." Nathaniel nodded and fixed his gaze again on the sea. The clouds had cleared, and a thin moon shone on the waves.

"Douglas! Moss! How goes the watch?" came a shout from below.

Nathaniel looked down. There on the deck stood Mr. Turner. "It goes well, sir!" the boy shouted in reply.

"Aye, well indeed!" yelled the blacksmith. "The boy is a good companion and able-bodied as any man on board. I wouldn't have gotten the main sail furled without his help." Satisfied with the report, Mr. Turner walked away.

Able-bodied as any man on board. Mr. Douglas's words rang in Nathaniel's head. It was high praise, but the cabin boy was eager to believe he had earned it.

Nathaniel straightened up. The worst of the storm was over. The sea still swelled, but the moon held tight to the sky. For the first time since he left home, Nathaniel felt like a whaleman.

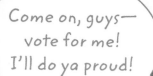

Impress ME!

Come on, guys—vote for me! I'll do ya proud!

Please consider voting for me. I'll work very hard to represent you.

In some settings, you may not worry about making a good impression. When you're chatting with friends and family, you talk in a way that is very casual. When you speak to people you want to impress, you should speak more formally. You can say almost the same thing using **formal language** as you can by using **informal language**.

Copy the chart below onto a separate sheet of paper. Read each row. Fill in the empty box by changing the words to formal or informal language.

Informal	Formal
?	He will be grateful if you can assist him.
Awesome story!	?
The kid Nathaniel was pretty proud of himself.	?
?	I think I would have a difficult time living on that ship.

What's Your Role?

Small-group discussions are a great way to communicate ideas and make decisions. If a discussion is not organized, however, good thoughts and ideas can easily get lost. Having defined roles in a discussion is one way to stay on topic and make sure that everyone participates. Read the group discussion roles and responsibilities described below.

Timekeeper:
"I make sure we watch the time and stay on topic."

Recorder:
"I take notes about the important things we say."

Leader:
"I direct the discussion and make sure everyone is heard."

Group member:
"I participate in the discussion by sharing what I think."

Presenter:
"I use the recorder's notes and tell the class what we talked about."

Follow the directions to have a discussion with your classmates.

1. Form small groups of about six students.

2. Imagine that you are part of a student committee that wants to find ways to improve school life.

3. As a group, choose your roles. Then decide on a topic such as lunch choices or homework policy. Begin your discussion. Be sure to listen carefully and respond politely.

4. Help the presenter prepare to share the group's ideas with the class.

Your Turn Storytelling at Its BEST

A narrative is a piece of writing that tells a story. The purpose of a narrative is to entertain your readers. Your audience could be your friends, your family, or anyone else who enjoys a good story.

When you write, you want the ending of your stories to be powerful and leave your audience satisfied. A strong ending ties everything together, and readers close the book knowing why the characters felt and acted as they did.

Reread the ending of "A Storm at Sea" shown below. What did you think of it? Were you satisfied with the way the story ended? What would you have changed? Why?

Able-bodied as any man on board. Mr. Douglas's words rang in Nathaniel's head. It was high praise, but the cabin boy was eager to believe he had earned it.

Nathaniel straightened up. The worst of the storm was over. The sea still swelled, but the moon held tight to the sky. For the first time since he left home, Nathaniel felt like a whaleman.

REFLECT ON YOUR WRITING

Choose a fictional story that you've recently written. Reread it. Then reread it again, thinking about the ending. Ask yourself:

- Does my ending tie everything together?
- How do I feel after I read my ending?
- Have I left my readers unsure about anything that happened in the story?

Work on revising the ending of your story until you're certain that you've done the best job you can.

Story Rewind

Now find a short story from your classroom library. Think about how you might rewind the ending of the story by changing or improving it. Rewrite the ending in a way that you think would be stronger or more satisfying. Share your new ending and the reasons for your changes with a partner.

INVASION from MARS

a radio play by Howard Koch
illustrated by JT Morrow

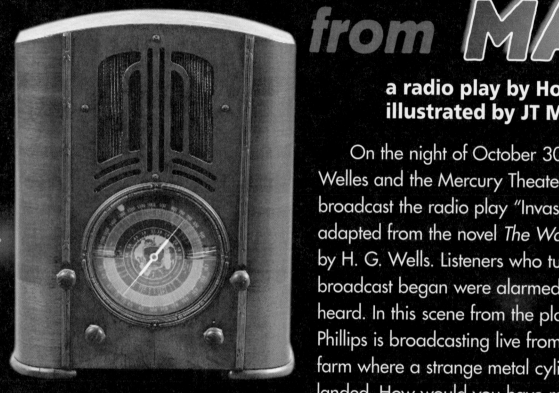

On the night of October 30, 1938, Orson Welles and the Mercury Theater Company broadcast the radio play "Invasion from Mars," adapted from the novel *The War of the Worlds* by H. G. Wells. Listeners who tuned in after the broadcast began were alarmed by what they heard. In this scene from the play, newsman Carl Phillips is broadcasting live from the New Jersey farm where a strange metal cylinder has crash-landed. How would you have reacted to hearing these words on your radio?

Phillips: Well, I've never seen anything like it. The color is sort of yellowish-white. Curious spectators now are pressing close to the object in spite of the efforts of the police to keep them back. They're getting in front of my line of vision. Would you mind standing on one side, please?

Policeman: One side, there, one side.

Phillips: While the policemen are pushing the crowd back, here's Mr. Wilmuth, owner of the farm here. He may have some interesting facts to add. . . . Mr. Wilmuth, would you please tell the radio audience as much as you remember of this rather unusual visitor that dropped in your backyard? Step closer, please. Ladies and gentlemen, this is Mr. Wilmuth.

Wilmuth: I was listenin' to the radio.

Phillips: Closer and louder, please.

Wilmuth: Pardon me!

Phillips: Louder, please, and closer.

Wilmuth: Yes, sir—while I was listening to the radio and kinda drowsin', that Professor fellow was talkin' about Mars, so I was half dozin' and half . . .

Phillips: Yes, Mr. Wilmuth. Then what happened?

Wilmuth: As I was sayin', I was listenin' to the radio kinda halfways . . .

Phillips: Yes, Mr. Wilmuth, and then you saw something?

Wilmuth: Not first off. I heard something.

Phillips: And what did you hear?

Wilmuth: A hissing sound. Like this: sssssss . . . kinda like a fourt' of July rocket.

Phillips: Then what?

Wilmuth: Turned my head out the window and would have swore I was to sleep and dreamin'.

Phillips: Yes?

Wilmuth: I seen a kinda greenish streak and then zingo! Somethin' smacked the ground. Knocked me clear out of my chair!

Phillips: Well, were you frightened, Mr. Wilmuth?

Wilmuth: Well, I — I ain't quite sure. I reckon I — I was kinda riled.

Phillips: Thank you, Mr. Wilmuth. Thank you.

Wilmuth: Want me to tell you some more?

Phillips: No . . . That's quite all right, that's plenty.

Phillips: Ladies and gentlemen, you've just heard Mr. Wilmuth, owner of the farm where this thing has fallen. I wish I could convey the atmosphere . . . the background of this . . . fantastic scene. Hundreds of cars are parked in a field in back of us. Police are trying to rope off the roadway leading into the farm. But it's no use. They're breaking right through. Their headlights throw an enormous spot on the pit where the object's half buried. Some of the more daring souls are venturing near the edge. Their silhouettes stand out against the metal sheen.

(Faint humming sound)

One man wants to touch the thing . . . he's having an argument with a policeman. The policeman wins. . . . Now, ladies and gentlemen, there's something I haven't mentioned in all this excitement, but it's becoming more distinct. Perhaps you've caught it already on your radio. Listen: *(Long pause)* . . .

Do you hear it? It's a curious humming sound that seems to come from inside the object. I'll move the microphone nearer. Here. *(Pause)* Now we're not more than twenty-five feet away. Can you hear it now? Oh, Professor Pierson!

Pierson: Yes, Mr. Phillips?

Phillips: Can you tell us the meaning of that scraping noise inside the thing?

Pierson: Possibly the unequal cooling of its surface.

Phillips: Do you still think it's a meteor, Professor?

Pierson: I don't know what to think. The metal casing is definitely extraterrestrial . . . not found on this earth. Friction with the earth's atmosphere usually tears holes in a meteorite. This thing is smooth and, as you can see, of cylindrical shape.

Phillips: Just a minute! Something's happening! Ladies and gentlemen, this is terrific! This end of the thing is beginning to flake off! The top is beginning to rotate like a screw! The thing must be hollow!

Voices: She's a movin'!

Look, the darn thing's unscrewing!

Keep back, there! Keep back, I tell you!

Maybe there's men in it trying to escape!

It's red hot, they'll burn to a cinder!

Keep back there. Keep those idiots back!

(*Suddenly the clanking sound of a huge piece of falling metal*)

Voices: She's off! The top's loose!

Look out there! Stand back!

Phillips: Ladies and gentlemen, this is the most terrifying thing I have ever witnessed . . . Wait a minute! *Someone's crawling out of the hollow top.* Someone or . . . something. I can see peering out of that black hole two luminous disks . . . are they eyes? It might be a face. It might be . . .

(Shout of awe from the crowd)

Phillips: Good heavens, something's wriggling out of the shadow like a gray snake. Now it's another one, and another. They look like tentacles to me. There, I can see the thing's body. It's large as a bear and it glistens like wet leather. But that face. It . . . it's indescribable. I can hardly force myself to keep looking at it. The eyes are black and gleam like a serpent. The mouth is V-shaped with saliva dripping from its rimless lips that seem to quiver and pulsate. The monster or whatever it is can hardly move. It seems weighed down by . . . possibly gravity or something. The thing's raising up. The crowd falls back. They've seen enough. This is the most extraordinary experience. I can't find words . . . I'm pulling this microphone with me as I talk. I'll have to stop the description until I've taken a new position. Hold on, will you please, I'll be back in a minute.

(Fade into piano)

Announcer Two: We are bringing you an eyewitness account of what's happening on the Wilmuth farm, Grovers Mill, New Jersey. *(More piano)* We now return you to Carl Phillips at Grovers Mill.

Phillips: Ladies and gentlemen (Am I on?). Ladies and gentlemen, here I am, back of a stone wall that adjoins Mr. Wilmuth's garden. From here I get a sweep of the whole scene. I'll give you every detail as long as I can talk. As long as I can see. More state police have arrived. They're drawing up a cordon in front of the pit, about thirty of them. No need to push the crowd back now. They're willing to keep their distance. The captain is conferring with someone. We can't quite see who. Oh yes, I believe it's Professor Pierson. Yes, it is. Now they've parted. The professor moves around one side, studying the object, while the captain and two policemen advance with something in their hands. I can see it now. It's a white handkerchief tied to a pole . . . a flag of truce. If those creatures know what that means . . . what anything means! . . . *Wait!* Something's happening!

(Hissing sound followed by a humming that increases in intensity)

A humped shape is rising out of the pit. I can make out a small beam of light against a mirror. What's that? There's a jet of flame springing from that mirror, and it leaps right at the advancing men. It strikes them head on! Good Lord, they're turning into flame!

(Screams and unearthly shrieks)

Now the whole field's caught fire. *(Explosion)* The woods . . . the barns . . . the gas tanks of automobiles . . . it's spreading everywhere. It's coming this way. About twenty yards to my right . . .

(Crash of microphone . . . then dead silence)

The Best Way to Say It

With hundreds of thousands of words in the English language from which to choose, why use *nice* when you can write *lovely* or *fantastic*? Dull, ordinary words like *nice* paint a picture in the reader's mind that is fuzzy and without precise details. On the other hand, exact words create strong, clear images in the reader's mind. When you write, try to paint an interesting picture for readers with precise, exact words!

For **shout**, try *bellow, holler,* or *roar.*
For **walk**, try *stroll, march,* or *hike.*
For **loud**, try *blaring, thunderous,* or *booming.*

Look at the pictures and read the captions on the next page. Then choose the most precise word that fits in the blank to complete the sentence.

After hearing the "Invasion from Mars" radio broadcast in 1938, some listeners worried that ___?___ aliens had actually landed in New Jersey. *(bad, hostile)*

The dog ___?___ under the bed when he heard the roaring space rocket. *(bolted, went)*

"Can we please stay at the exhibit longer?" Julian ___?___. *(pleaded, asked)*

Sheila looked ___?___ when her teacher chose her story to enter in the science fiction contest. *(happy, overjoyed)*

If you want to describe something that is *difficult*, the words *exhausting, complex,* and *puzzling* may communicate your idea more precisely. Which word would you use to describe each situation below? Discuss your answers with a partner.

- a mystery that no one can solve
- putting together a model that has many small parts
- a steep hike up a mountain

Your Turn — Link It Up!

When you share your opinion in writing, you want readers to agree with your views and believe what you say. Linking your opinion to strong reasons will help to persuade your audience. How might you use the transition words and phrases below to show reasons supporting an opinion?

for instance   **in order to**   **therefore**   **in addition**   **including**

After you have explained the reasons for your opinion, provide a concluding statement that restates the opinion in a memorable way. Leave readers with something to think about! How did the writer of the movie review below use transition words and phrases? What makes his conclusion strong?

| File | Edit | View | Favorites | Tools | Help |

Josh's Blog

Movie Review

This week's new movie, *Treasure Chance*, is not perfect, but I recommend that you see it. While the story is entertaining, the action is not always realistic. For instance, when Gigi jumps from one building to another, her legs do not seem nearly long enough to reach across the openings. In addition, the character Luca is not believable when he lifts the boulder covering the treasure chest. If you can ignore these flaws, look forward to a thrilling adventure story. Put this one on your "must see" list!

Josh Crawford

Center Street School

Grade 4

Post a comment

Reflect on Your Writing

Choose a piece of writing in which you have expressed an opinion. Does it include all the important parts of opinion writing? Ask yourself:

- Did I state an opinion?
- Did I include reasons for my opinion?
- Did I use transition words and phrases to link opinions and reasons?
- Is my conclusion strong, and does it give readers something to think about?

Add transition words or phrases to the piece of opinion writing you have chosen. Be sure your conclusion says something that readers will remember.

Cold, Cold Science

by Dewey Badeaux

At Palmer Station in Antarctica, scientists live and work in a world of ice. A giant ice sheet that covers the continent helps scientists at Palmer Station understand an environment that doesn't exist anywhere else on Earth.

Palmer Station

Home Away from Home

Palmer Station is one of three bases in Antarctica operated by the United States. It is located on Anvers Island, just west of the Antarctic Peninsula in the northwestern part of the continent. Scientists at Palmer Station live at the base year-round and perform field studies in the surrounding environment. One visiting writer, Kate Madin, said, "This town has a single purpose, and everyone here is a part of it: scientific research on the Antarctic coastal ecosystem."

Ninety percent of our planet's ice is found in Antarctica.

Frozen Sculptures

The unique features of the Antarctic landscape give the scientists at Palmer Station many frozen clues to use in their research. Antarctica is glacier country. A glacier is a mass of ice and snow formed on land over thousands of years. A glacier slowly moves across land due to gravity and its great weight. The Antarctic ice sheet, an enormous glacier, covers 98 percent of the continent and contains approximately 5 million square miles of ice, averaging 7,000 feet thick. The Antarctic ice sheet is the largest single mass of ice on Earth, and it contains about 70 percent of Earth's freshwater.

Nearly half of Antarctica's coastline is made up of thick, floating ice called ice shelves. Ice shelves result from the Antarctic ice sheet's movement towards the coastline. They form where the ice sheet meets the water. Palmer Station is located near the Larsen Ice Shelf.

Icebergs can be seen in the frigid waters near Antarctica's coast. An iceberg is a large mass of floating ice broken off from a glacier or ice shelf. Icebergs can be the size of an automobile or a small country! An iceberg's movement is influenced by ocean currents and winds. Eventually, icebergs melt and disappear.

Scientists at Palmer Station study how the Antarctic ice sheet moves and how the temperature of the ocean changes over time. They learn how changes to the ice sheet and ice shelves affect animals that live in Antarctica. The scientists' work also helps them understand how changes in Earth's climate can impact the rest of the world.

Scientists at Palmer Station believe that many icebergs came from the Wilkins Ice Shelf when it broke apart in 2008.

Antarctic winds can reach speeds of 185 miles per hour!

Windiest, Driest, Coldest

Antarctica is a place of climate extremes. Did you know that it is the windiest place on Earth? During a blizzard, the wind in Antarctica is so strong that it can change the shape of ice and rocks. The strongest winds are found along the coast of the continent and on the Antarctic Peninsula.

Antarctica may not be hot, but much of the continent is the driest place on Earth. It is a desert! Because the air is so cold and dry, it is hard for clouds to form and make rain or snow in the central part of the continent. Not only is Antarctica the world's driest desert, it's also the largest!

The temperature in Antarctica's interior during the winter can get as cold as –94° F. However, in summer, the temperature along the Antarctic Peninsula can climb to almost 60° F. Because the conditions in Antarctica can be so harsh, scientists are very busy there during the warmer summer season. During certain weeks in summer, the sun does not set at all—there is daylight 24 hours a day! The warm temperatures cause the ice along the coast to melt and can impact Antarctica's wildlife.

Antarctica's Wildlife

Zoologists are scientists who study wildlife, from very small to very large. At Palmer Station, scientists measure temperatures on the coast and in the ocean. They also get information from satellites that orbit the earth. This information helps zoologists learn how changes in climate affect the krill, seabirds, and other animals that make up Antarctica's ecosystem.

Krill live in the seas surrounding Antarctica. Similar to shrimp in size and structure, an individual Antarctic krill is about 2 inches long. Krill is an important source of food for much larger fish, birds, and mammals. Thousands of krill swim together in swarms, making it easy for whales, seals, and penguins to catch them.

Dragonfish, cod, and icefish live in the Southern Ocean, which surrounds Antarctica. These fish species mainly live at the bottom of the ocean and feed on krill and other creatures. Starfish, squid, and sea spiders live in the Southern Ocean as well.

Swarm of krill

Seals can be found relaxing in the cold waters of Antarctica. Of the many different types of seals in Antarctica, the elephant seal is the largest. A male elephant seal can weigh up to 8,000 lbs. Many scientists believe that seals are most similar to otters and skunks. On the other hand, other scientists believe seals are more closely related to bears!

Seals are able to hold their breath for a long time while swimming underwater. Some seals can swim up to 50 miles a day when they are hunting for krill, fish, and penguins.

Enormous whales live in the Southern Ocean, too. Like other mammals, whales need air to live. Most mammals, such as seals, breathe through their noses and mouths. Whales, however, breathe through an opening on the top of their heads. Humpbacks, orcas, and many other types of whales can be seen in the icy seas of Antarctica.

Elephant seal

Humpback whale

Different kinds of seabirds call Antarctica home. They live and nest on Antarctica's shores and look for food in the water. The albatross is one kind of seabird that lives in Antarctica. It has a wingspan of 11 feet, making it the largest flying bird in the world.

Penguins, another kind of seabird, live and nest in large groups. Unlike other seabirds, these black and white birds cannot fly. Penguins walk on land and swim in the Southern Ocean to look for food.

At Palmer Station, scientists are very interested in penguins. These scientists study how the sun, atmosphere, ocean, and food supply cause the penguin population to rise or fall. Because Antarctica is so isolated, scientists can focus on a single species and learn a lot about how that species survives.

Emperor penguins

Looking Back and to the Future

Fossils discovered on the islands near the Antarctic Peninsula have led many scientists to believe that Antarctica was once a much warmer place, where small, bird-like dinosaurs roamed the land. Fossils of ancient trees also suggest it was warm enough for flowers to bloom. Can you imagine Antarctica warm and sunny?

Too much sun, of course, is a problem. Scientists have discovered a hole in the ozone layer in the atmosphere above Antarctica. The ozone layer is a gaseous shield that protects us from the sun's powerful rays. Without this protection, most life on Earth could not survive. To help shrink the ozone hole, governments in many countries are teaming up to decrease pollution. In time, scientists believe this will help solve the problem.

The work that scientists do at Palmer Station allows people around the world to learn about our planet's climate, oceans, and animal life. By studying clues from the past and what is happening today, they also uncover information that helps us make important predictions about the future.

Scientists take an ice sample for their research.

Activity Central

Wild About Words

The e-mail below contains some words about science that you may not know very well. As you read the e-mail, think about what the words mean and how you can learn more about them.

File	Edit	View	Favorites	Tools	Help

Search

To: Cory

From: Nathan

Subject: I made it to Antarctica

Hi Cory!

How are you? After three days of traveling, I finally made it to Antarctica! Tomorrow I'm joining a group of **zoologists** to look for wildlife. They promised to show me penguins and seals living along the coast. I'm glad the scientists are learning how to protect some of the **endangered** animals here. Later, we will actually walk on a glacier. That should be fun!

I've met some **geologists**, too. They are studying Antarctica's ice and soil. I'll write you again soon about my next adventure!

Bye for now,
Nathan

Choose a boldface word from the e-mail. On a separate sheet of paper, make a word web like the one shown here to explain what the word means. Use context clues, a dictionary, or reference sources to help you.

large mass of ice

moves slowly

glacier

forms over thousands of years

climate causes it to grow and shrink

Don't Confuse Me

Some words sound alike but have different spellings and meanings. Look below at the examples of words that can be easily confused if you are not paying attention!

Word	Meaning
weather	climate
whether	shows choice or doubt between two things
hear	to listen to
here	in this place

Use the examples above to start a list of words that can be easily confused. Add other words you know to the list. For each word, include a description, a sentence, or a picture to help you remember how to use the word correctly. Add to the list when you come across new words in speaking or in writing.

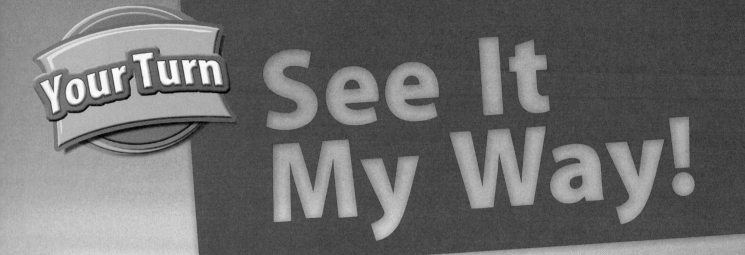

See It My Way!

In persuasive writing, you try to convince an audience that your opinion is correct. Make your opinion clear in an opening statement. Then provide reasons for your opinion. Use facts, details, and quotations to support the reasons for your argument.

- **Facts** are true statements and can be proved.
- **Details** give more information about facts.
- **Quotations** from an expert help to convince readers that your opinion is valid.

Example

Opinion: Scientists have a responsibility to educate people about the ocean.

Reason 1: Without scientists, the underwater world would be a mystery to many people.

Fact: Scientists have discovered that oceans are a complex community made up of many living things.

Detail: Some scientists have studied how ocean plants and animals feed on each other to get energy and nutrition.

Quotation: A marine biologist said, "All of the ocean's plants and animals play an important role in the marine ecosystem."

Reflect on Your Writing

Choose a persuasive essay you have written or another opinion piece that shows your strong feelings about a topic. Make sure you have done the best job you can to convince readers to agree with your opinion. Ask yourself:

Have I

- stated a clear opinion that shows how I feel about the topic?

- included reasons to support my opinion?

- included facts, details, and quotations to explain the reasons in my argument?

Add facts, details, and quotations to the piece of persuasive writing you have chosen.

What Is a Myth?

A myth is a traditional story that explains how something in the world began or came to be. The characters may be gods and goddesses, monsters, and strange creatures who can do impossible things.

HERCULES' QUEST

retold by Martina Melendez   illustrated by David Harrington

It was fortunate for the hero Hercules (HER•kyoo•leez) that he was born in the winter. He had plenty of time to gain strength to fight serpents the following spring. The angry goddess Hera dropped the serpents into the baby's cradle. They slithered through baby Hercules' blankets, hissed at him, and prepared to strike.

Hercules laughed at the silly snakes, coiled up like piles of rope. He laughed at their silly noises. Then he killed them with his bare hands.

It was clear that Hercules was no ordinary baby boy. He was the son of Zeus, king of the gods. It was unlucky for Hercules, however, that Hera was jealous of her husband's affection for his son. Hera wanted Zeus' attention on her. When the snakes failed to hurt Hercules, she came up with another plan.

"I'll have him use his strength for harm," the goddess said to herself. "Then Zeus will punish the boy himself."

Hera successfully used her power on Hercules. Zeus was disappointed at his son's behavior, and so he decided that Hercules would have to earn back his honor and prove worthy of the gift of strength.

Zeus ordered Hercules to serve King Eurystheus (yoo•RIS•thee•us). Many dangerous enemies lived near Eurystheus' kingdom, and a strong boy like Hercules could keep his people safe.

However, Hera had other things in mind for Hercules. To be sure that Hercules would be out of the way for a long time, she gave Eurystheus ideas for tasks that Hercules could never complete.

Hercules went to live among the herdsmen and cattle in Eurystheus' kingdom. A fierce, evil lion lived nearby in the valley of Nemea (NEE•me•uh).

"Your first task," said King Eurystheus, "is to kill the Nemean lion."

The impossible mission was Hera's idea, of course. The lion had claws like gleaming swords and teeth even sharper. It could eat a herd of antelope for breakfast and a small boy in a single bite.

After accepting the challenge, Hercules watched and waited for the lion to come out of the forest. "The lion may be strong, but I am stronger," Hercules boasted. "I fought serpents when I was a baby. I killed them with my hands."

When the lion emerged, Hercules first tried to kill the lion with his mighty club. When that failed, he tried to kill the lion with razor-sharp spears. No weapons would harm the beast! So, the boy wrapped his arms around the lion's neck. Hercules had killed serpents barehanded, and he killed the lion with his bare hands, too.

Hercules beamed with pride as the lion lay dead at his feet. He lifted the heavy body and paraded it through the land. The people cheered and hollered. They praised Hercules for his strength. Zeus smiled from his throne on Olympus, while Hera stewed from behind a cloud.

"Well, well," she thought. "Now what idea can I give Eurystheus?" Then she remembered that the Hydra of Argos lived nearby. The Hydra was a monster with nine heads, and one head was immortal. Like anything else immortal, that head could not be destroyed. Hercules had strangled the Nemean lion, but could he destroy the Hydra?

"You *must* kill the Hydra to keep my kingdom safe," ordered Eurystheus. Bravely, Hercules accepted the task.

He shot flaming arrows at the Hydra, but the Hydra coiled around Hercules' leg. He hit the Hydra's heads with a club. For every head destroyed, two more grew in its place!

Finally, Hercules triumphed over all the heads but one. Then, with a little help from Zeus, he destroyed the immortal head at last. Hera was *really* angry now!

"In no time at all, that boy will be back in Zeus' good graces!" she hissed. "I must stop him!" Her angry howls rattled Mount Olympus. Her heavy stomps broke holes through the clouds.

After storming and stomping for hours, Hera came up with a plan. This plan, she felt certain, could not possibly fail. Hera told Eurystheus that he must order Hercules to bring him some apples. Of course, the apples were not ordinary. They were made of gold and grew on trees in the Garden of the Hesperides (hes•PAIR•uh•deez), and a fierce dragon kept watch over the trees.

"I'm not afraid of that dragon," declared Hercules. "I killed the Nemean lion and the Hydra of Argos. I'll kill the dragon while he's sleeping."

When Hercules approached the garden, the dragon was sleeping, just as Hercules had hoped. Upon hearing the boy's footsteps, however, the dragon opened one eye to peek at his unwanted guest.

Hercules approached the creature, which lay coiled among the trees. The apples hung from the trees' branches. The branches hung over the dragon's head.

Hercules devised a plan. "I'll ask Atlas to get me the apples," he said with confidence. Atlas owned the Garden of the Hesperides, and the dragon worked for him.

Hercules walked for weeks to reach the Mountain of Atlas. Atlas had been sent there long ago as punishment from the gods. Atlas was doomed to spend his life holding the weight of the world on his shoulders. "Perhaps," thought Hercules, "Atlas could use some help."

"Poor Atlas," said Hercules. "You must be so tired. Won't you let me carry your load for you a while? I am strong enough to do it."

Atlas was overjoyed! He could hardly believe his ears! He dreamed about walking the earth and smelling the flowers once again. He longed to wade through rivers and streams.

"I'll be happy to give you a rest," Hercules told Atlas, "if you'll do one little thing for me. Bring me some apples from the Garden of the Hesperides."

Atlas agreed and left promptly. He walked joyfully over the land.

Before too long, Atlas returned. He placed the apples before Hercules, thanked him kindly, and prepared to go on his way.

"The apples are not for me," explained Hercules. "I must take them to King Eurystheus."

"I'll take the apples to him for you," said Atlas, who had tasted freedom and wanted more of it. Hercules was sure he would never return.

"Oh, would you *please* take them for me?" Hercules begged without missing a beat. "I would be forever grateful. But I am not as used to this load as you are, and my arms have grown tired and stiff. Would you relieve me for just a minute while I take a little rest?"

Atlas shrugged his shoulders. "Okay, just for a moment, and then I will personally deliver your apples for you," he said. He handed Hercules the apples and took back the weight of the world.

Hercules stretched his weary shoulders. He stretched his arms and legs. Then he bid Atlas a fond farewell and left for Eurystheus' palace.

"Well, well," said Eurystheus when Hercules gave him the golden apples. "You are not only strong, but clever. You've accomplished yet another impossible task."

Now, Eurystheus was a powerful king, but Zeus was a powerful god. Zeus had the power to grant the gift of strength, and he had the power to take it away. From that day on, Hercules promised to use his strength only to help others. He treated people respectfully and acted kindly at all times.

Zeus was pleased with his son Hercules and rewarded him. He brought his son to Mount Olympus to live among the gods. Hercules was now immortal and lived forever on Olympus with a duty to protect the mortals below.

What Is a Folktale?

A folktale is a story that has been handed down in a community from one generation to the next. The characters are often animals who talk and act like people, and the plot often teaches a lesson about life.

ZOMO'S FRIENDS

retold by Tamara Andrews
illustrated by Benjamin Bay

The best way to have a friend is to be one. Zomo the Rabbit didn't know that—he had to learn it for himself. Many animals lived in the jungle, and many were good friends to one another. Zomo thought he was better than all the other animals, and he certainly thought he was more clever. He was the cleverest animal in the jungle. He was the cleverest animal in the land.

Zomo was quite proud of his cleverness. He often boasted and bragged to the other animals, and he laughed at his own many tricks. But as much as Zomo liked being clever, he was not happy. The animals were tired of Zomo's boasting and bragging. Not one of them wanted to be Zomo's friend.

So Zomo the Rabbit went to talk to Sky God for advice. He waited at the big rock in the jungle where he knew Sky God often appeared.

"Hey, Croc!" shouted Zomo. "It's morning! Don't you think it's time to wake up?" Crocodile opened his eyes angrily. The last thing he wanted to see was Zomo. He took one look and snapped his eyes shut.

"I have a story to tell you," said Zomo. "It's really a beautiful tale." He started talking, but Croc kept his eyes shut. Zomo shared the tale of Zebra and the rain dance. He told about how Zebra's dancing made the rain fall from the clouds. Finally, Croc began to listen, wide awake!

"Aha! I have your attention," said Zomo. "Now I can show you the dance." Zomo began to dance, but not like he danced with Zebra. He did not glide—he hopped. He did not sway— he fell. He fell into the water near Crocodile. His hat landed upside down.

Crocodile laughed and laughed. Zomo began laughing, too. Crocodile laughed so hard he cried big crocodile tears. The tears dripped from his eyes and fell into Zomo's hat.

Zomo felt very clever indeed. He waved goodbye to Crocodile and walked the long way back to Sky God. Once again, Sky God was impressed.

"So now you have a friend in the grasslands," said Sky God. "You have Crocodile's friendship, too. You made them smile and laugh, but these animals are not happy. They won't be happy at all until someone brings back the Moon."

Zomo had forgotten about the Moon. The Moon had been stolen years ago, and the night sky had grown very dark. "I brought back the tale of Zebra," thought Zomo. "I brought back Crocodile's tears, too. I can bring back the Moon—I know it. I am the cleverest animal in the jungle. I am the cleverest animal in all the land."

Zomo set out once again, this time to look for the Moon. He walked deep into the jungle and searched for the deepest ditch. Before long, he found it. He peered inside, and just as he suspected, he saw a faint white ball glowing beneath the dirt.

Zomo wasted no time. He was sure he had found the Moon. He tipped over his hat, which was quite heavy with Croc's tears, and emptied it into the ditch. As the water in the ditch got higher and higher, the Moon floated to the surface. Zomo lifted it from the water and tossed it up in the sky.

The animals came out from their hidden homes in the jungle. One by one, they looked up at the sky. Suddenly, the animals began shouting! "Hooray for Zomo!" shouted Casey the Camel. "Friend to us all," said Glinda the Goat.

Zomo felt more clever than ever. He felt better than ever, too. It was great to be clever, but it was even better to have friends. It seemed all of the animals were now Zomo's friends. He remembered an old saying that was kind of clever: *You can never have enough friends.*

WHAT'S IN A NAME?

Myths may be centuries old, but we still remember many of their characters in the words we use today. Hercules was extremely strong, so we say that something requiring great strength or effort is a Herculean task. Read the description of the character Tantalus below. What do you think *tantalize* means?

Tantalus: As punishment for his pride and other crimes, Tantalus was placed in neck-deep water that he could not reach when he tried to drink. Above him hung fruit that moved out of reach when he tried to eat.

tantalize, tantalizing

Read the paragraph below. Determine the meaning of each myth-based word or phrase in boldface. Use print and online sources to help you with the meanings. Think about how reading myths can help you understand what the words mean.

Getting the yard ready for tonight's party all by myself is a **Herculean** task. The idea of playing ball instead is **tantalizing**. To move the clubhouse and swing set, I'll need **Olympian** strength. I may feel the **wrath of Hera** from Mom if I don't do a decent job. If I get it done on time, though, the party will be a great success.

WISE WORDS

Adages and proverbs are memorable sayings that have been used for a long time. In just a few words, they explain little lessons about life that many people find to be true. What do you think the adages and proverbs to the right mean? How could you use the lessons in your own life?

Words of Wisdom in Stories

Folktales often share words of wisdom. Reread the story "Zomo's Friends." Try to find words of wisdom that might be famous adages or proverbs. With a partner, discuss what the sayings mean to you. Then try to write a new adage or proverb based on the story.

A penny saved is a penny earned.

A closed mouth catches no flies.

Bring Your Story Home

The heroes in both "Hercules' Quest" and "Zomo's Friends" are called to adventure. They are asked to do impossible tasks. A reader may ask: *Why are these tasks important? What do Hercules and Zomo learn from their successes?* The conclusion to each story brings all the important events to a satisfying end.

In a personal narrative, the conclusion is very special because you are telling about events that really happened to *you*! Bring the reader "home" by explaining what made your experience important or what you learned from it. A strong ending gives meaning to your actions. Don't be shy about sharing your thoughts or describing your feelings!

I fidgeted impatiently, waiting for the plane to land. Visiting my friends had been fun, but it also made me appreciate the comforts of home. Thinking about talking with my parents and seeing my younger brother after two weeks away made me smile. My first trip away from home was the last one I hoped to take for a long time.

Reflect on Your Writing

Choose a personal narrative that you have recently written. Then reread it, thinking about the ending. Ask yourself:

▶ Have I explained why the events in the narrative are important?

▶ Did I include thoughts and feelings about my experiences?

▶ Did I leave the reader feeling satisfied?

Rewrite your concluding paragraph to make sure it includes the elements of a good conclusion. Then discuss your conclusion with a partner.

Exploring and Building Pyramids

by Orli Zuravicky

What kind of building do you find most interesting? Maybe it is a skyscraper in the city or a pyramid in the desert. Have you ever wondered what happens between getting an idea for a building and starting to build it? One important step is creating a model of the building.

What Is a Three-Dimensional Model?

Sometimes it's hard to imagine how something looks without seeing it in front of you. Architects make drawings and models of the buildings they design before they are built. These models help them make the buildings properly, so that the buildings will stand straight and last for a long time.

Anyone can build a model. Models help us to understand things about a shape that a drawing can't show us.

Flat shapes, like a triangle or a square, have two measurable dimensions: length and width. They are called two-dimensional, or 2-D, shapes. A cube is a three-dimensional, or 3-D, shape. The dimensions of a 3-D shape are known as height, width, and depth. Height is the distance from the top to the bottom of an object. Depth is the distance from the front to the back of an object.

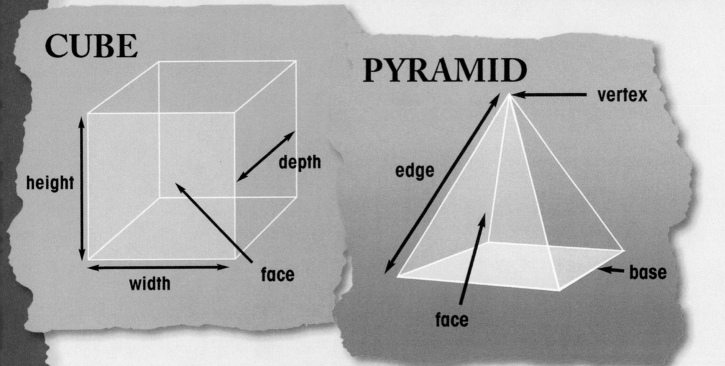

A pyramid is also a three-dimensional shape. Pyramids, cubes, and most other 3-D shapes have sides called *faces.* Faces are flat surfaces that meet at the edges of the shape. The point, or corner, where three or more edges meet is called a *vertex.* The *base* is the bottom of the object. In order to create a 3-D model of a shape, you need to know how many faces it has and the shapes of its faces and its base.

The Great Pyramids at Giza

Three of the world's most famous pyramids stand at a place in Egypt called Giza (GEE•zuh), near the city of Cairo (KY•roh). All three pyramids were built for famous Egyptian kings. One of these pyramids is called the Great Pyramid. It is the largest and most famous pyramid ever built! It was built for King Khufu, who ruled Egypt around 2500 B.C.

The Great Pyramid at Giza

The Great Pyramid is around 4,500 years old and was about 480 feet tall when it was first built. The Great Pyramid was the tallest structure in the world for over 43 centuries. It is made from over 2 million blocks of limestone and weighs around 5,750,000 tons! The pyramid is almost solid stone, but inside there are some hidden rooms, including the burial place of King Khufu. Next to the Great Pyramid stand the smaller pyramids built for two later kings named Khafre (KA•fruh) and Menkaure (men•KUHR•uh).

Let's make a model of the Great Pyramid. The Great Pyramid has a square base and four triangular faces. Using a ruler, draw a big square (at least 5 inches on each side) in the middle of a large piece of heavy construction paper. This will be the base of our model pyramid. With the ruler, draw 4 triangles that are 3 ½ inches tall, using the four edges of the square as bases for the triangles. These will be the faces of the pyramid. The sides of the triangles should be about 4 ¼ inches long.

Once you've drawn the base and all four faces of the pyramid, use scissors to cut along the edges of the four triangles. Don't cut the square base. Once you have cut the shape out, fold the four triangles up along the four lines of the square base. The triangles should meet each other at the top of the pyramid. Use tape to hold the four points together, and you have made a three-dimensional, or 3-D, model of the Great Pyramid at Giza!

3-D Model of the Great Pyramid

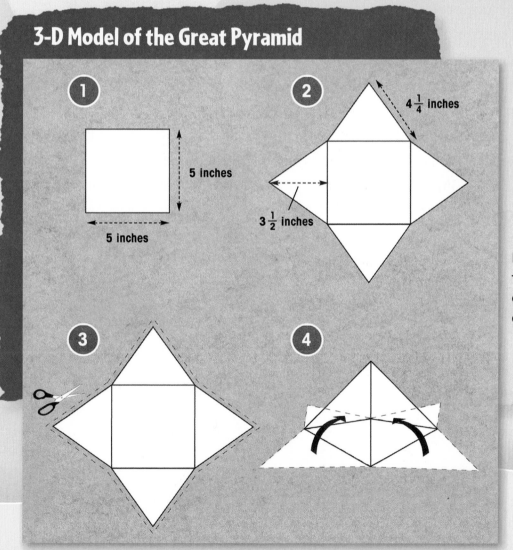

Make sure the two sides of each triangle are equal in length.

The Transamerica Building

Today's buildings are much different than the pyramids that were built centuries ago. Modern building materials and machinery have allowed architects to create buildings that are taller and bigger than the pyramids of long ago. In 1968, a man named John Beckett gave the United States its very own pyramid. One day Beckett noticed how beautifully the sun shone through the trees in a city park in San Francisco, California. He decided to create a building that would allow sunlight to reach the street below in the same way. Today, a modern pyramid stands in downtown San Francisco—the Transamerica Building. The Transamerica Building is made from stone, concrete, glass, and steel. It is 853 feet tall, almost twice the height of the Great Pyramid at Giza!

The Transamerica Building's shape means its 48 floors aren't of equal size. The largest floor is the 5th floor, which has 21,025 square feet. The 48th floor is the smallest, with 2,025 square feet. At the top of the building is the pyramid's tip, a 212-foot pointed roof covered in aluminum, a silver-colored metal that reflects the light from the sun.

An estimated 10,000 to 100,000 people were needed to build the Great Pyramid, and it probably took about 30 years to build. Because of modern machinery and materials, the Transamerica Building was built in less than three years by only about 1,500 people.

The Transamerica Building ▶

RA69

3-D Model of the Transamerica Building

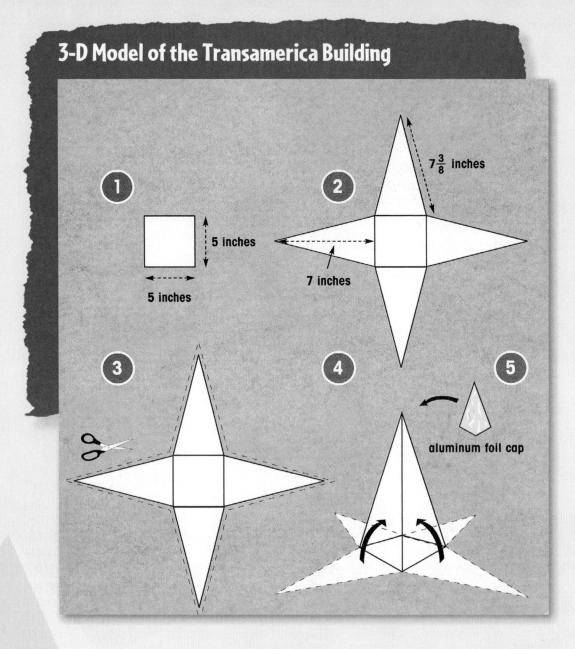

1

5 inches

5 inches

2

$7\frac{3}{8}$ inches

7 inches

3

4

5

aluminum foil cap

Make a basic 3-D model of the Transamerica Building by using the same instructions we used for the Great Pyramid. The Transamerica Building is steep, and its height is almost twice the height of the Great Pyramid, although its base is a little bit smaller. Following the Great Pyramid instructions, keep the base measurements the same, but double the height of the triangles. Finish by covering a small part of the top of the pyramid with aluminum foil to create the roof!

Now that you have learned about the pyramids of Egypt by making 3-D models, think of all the other things you can build! You can make a model of the Sears Tower (now the Willis Tower) in Chicago, the Eiffel Tower in France, or the Empire State Building in New York City! By learning how to build models of these things, you'll learn their history, how they were built, how tall they are, and many other interesting facts about them. What kind of model would you like to build?

◄ **The Willis Tower**

Pyramids:
Interactive Learning!

Most websites today are interactive. Links to maps, images, games, and related information make learning much more exciting. Below is an example of an interactive website. By clicking on the blue words in the article, the user would be taken to another page that gives more information.

File	Edit	View	Favorites	Tools	Help

Search

The Great Pyramid at Giza

About 4,500 years ago in ancient Egypt, the pharaoh King Khufu had an enormous pyramid built to house his tomb. Ancient Egyptians believed in an afterlife that was an actual place. To be prepared for this new life, a pharaoh needed his personal belongings. When a pharaoh died, these items, along with the king's mummy, were placed in the pyramid.

How was the pyramid built?

Over a period of 30 years, tens of thousands of skilled Egyptians labored to build the pyramid. When it was completed, the pyramid stood 480 feet high and weighed more than 5,750,000 tons. It was the tallest man-made structure in the world for centuries!

LINKS TO definition

pharaoh *(n)*: an ancient Egyptian ruler

LINKS TO images of a pharaoh's belongings

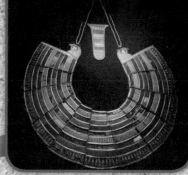

LINKS TO timeline of tall man-made structures

- Great Pyramid at Giza, **c. 2500 B.C.**

- Eiffel Tower, Paris, **1887**

- Empire State Building, New York, **1931**

- Willis Tower, Chicago, **1974**

When you paraphrase, you use your own words to restate information that you read or see. By paraphrasing, you can show that you have interpreted information correctly. Look at the map below. You can paraphrase the information in the map by explaining what you see.

Map

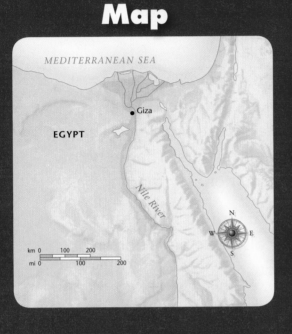

Paraphrase

The city of Giza is located on the Nile River near the Mediterranean Sea.

Read the information in the chart below. Tell a partner what the chart shows by paraphrasing the information. Then discuss what the chart helps you understand about giant constructions.

Giant Constructions

	Year Completed	Height
Great Pyramid at Giza	2500 B.C.	480 ft.
Eiffel Tower	1887 A.D.	1,052 ft.
Empire State Building	1931 A.D.	1,250 ft.
Willis Tower	1974 A.D.	1,454 ft.

Every Part Matters!

Things that have missing parts do not work well, or they may not work at all. Like a broken machine, written information that has missing parts can cause problems. Leaving out parts that matter will confuse your readers! The list below shows some important parts of informational writing.

- **Headings** break a long piece of writing into well-organized sections. They also give hints about the information in each section.

- **Transitions** are words and phrases that show how ideas are related. Transitions such as these are useful:

also	for example	because	next to
in addition	on the other hand		another

- **Precise words** help readers understand your ideas. Include definitions of words about a specific topic if you think readers won't understand what they mean.
- **Facts and quotations** make the topic come alive for readers and show that you have done research.
- The **conclusion** should remind readers about the most important things you have said about the topic.
- Consider using **illustrations and multimedia**. Visual and audio features will help others relate to the information.

Reflect on Your Writing

Choose the research report you have written or another informational piece with more than one paragraph. Does it have any missing parts? Ask yourself:

✿ Have I included headings to organize information?

✿ Have I used transitions to connect related sentences and paragraphs?

✿ Did I use definitions to explain words that readers may not know?

✿ Have I included facts and/or quotations to support my ideas?

✿ Did I include a strong conclusion that restates the most important ideas?

Revise the piece of informational writing that you have chosen until it has all the right working parts.

Present It!

Share your writing in an informative presentation. Use pictures, posters, and video or sound to make the information exciting for your audience. Be sure to practice how you will use everything in your presentation.

Paths to Discovery

In the next section of this magazine, you will discover that creepy things can be cool—especially spiders, frogs, turtles, and pythons. You'll learn how John Muir helped to create Yosemite National Park and how kids like you help to protect their own local habitats.

You'll read poems and articles about museums and nature, and you'll explore even more in lots of fun activities.

Your path to discovery begins when you turn the page!

Paths to Discovery

Lesson 26

1

The Girl Who Loved Spiders

I hate spiders. That's the first thing you should know about me.

My mom and I just moved from New York to Florida. That's the second thing you should know about me. We moved because my mom got a new teaching job at a university here.

Before we moved, my best friend, Billy, told me all kinds of creepy stories about spiders that live in Florida.

"My brother knows a guy from there who got bitten by a brown recluse spider," Billy said. "This guy was *smart* about spiders, too. He shook out his shoes. He watched his step. His bite healed, but it was the *worst*."

Mom has told me it takes three weeks to make a habit. It's only been a week since we moved, but I've already made one.

First thing every morning, I shake out my sneakers. Second thing, I put on my sneakers, though I'm still wearing pajamas. Third thing, I always watch my step.

Hey! Not one, but *three* new habits.

I blame them all on Billy.

I find Mom in the kitchen, drinking a glass of orange juice.

"You're awake, Luis? It's the crack of dawn!"

"Too hot."

Mom laughs. "It's summer. Aren't those winter pajamas?"

I don't tell her that flannel is better protection from spiders.

Over breakfast, Mom discusses her plan for the day. It's the same as yesterday's: unpack and settle in.

"Oh!" Mom sits up straight in her chair. "I found a dead scorpion yesterday. It was in perfect shape—not a leg missing. Fascinating, really. I saved it in case you wanted to see."

I gulp. "No thanks."

Great. Venomous spiders *and* scorpions.

Mom shrugs. "Okay. So what are you up to?"

"TV?"

Mom frowns.

"There's always the trampoline," I mutter.

Mom bought the trampoline the day after we arrived. It's as big and bouncy as can be—something I always wanted that Billy had. I just wish Billy were here now to teach me how to do a flip.

Not even 8:30 in the morning, and I'm on the trampoline again. Every jump takes me higher and higher.

In mid-air, I see her—two yards over—a girl about my age. I keep jumping. The girl kneels before a bush, in tall grass where all kinds of biting and stinging things might be. She stays very still.

Next jump, I see something in her hands . . . a pink ball?

Jump higher!

The girl claps the ball. Poof! A white cloud explodes from between her fingers.

I collapse onto the trampoline and scramble down. This I have to see. As I enter her yard, where the grass is taller, I freeze.

The ball in the girl's hands is a rolled-up sock. A camera dangles from a strap around her neck. She carefully settles the sock on the grass. Then she raises the camera and peers through it. I look where she's looking, at a delicate shape against the bush's leaves, like lace against green velvet.

The shape is a gigantic spider web, whitened by whatever the girl clapped from the sock.

Photographers sometimes make spider webs more visible by dusting them with cornstarch.

Not all spiders make their homes in webs. Some dig burrows.

"Yikes!" I yell at the sight of the web.

The girl cries out, surprised, and falls into the web. She springs up, web clinging to her. "What's the big idea?" she shouts.

"Um . . . I was warning you! Guess you don't know about brown recluse spiders?"

"Of course I do. I've been trying to find one. They're shy, like most arachnids. I've found rarer breeds, even the burrowing wolf spider. Still haven't tracked down a brown recluse." She points at the bush. "That was a common orb weaver. I've been watching her for days, until she got her web just

right." The girl glares. "It sure was pretty—until you came along. Who are you, anyway?"

"Luis. I just moved here."

"My name is Ashanti. Welcome to the neighborhood." She still sounds mad.

I cross my arms over my chest. "So you're on a spider safari. Why?"

"This summer my goal is to photograph one hundred spiders. I've always loved folktales about Anansi, a true spider-man. Spiders are cool."

I don't think before I say, "No, they aren't. Spiders are disgusting."

At that, Ashanti stalks away.

That afternoon Mom drives me to a park. "Never mind the heat," she says. "There'll be boys your age."

There's a decent playground, but a sign reads: BEWARE OF SNAKES! Where there are snakes, there must be spiders. Ashanti would be in heaven. As for me . . .

There are no boys my age. Two little girls sweat it out on the slide. Mom wilts on a bench. We drive home.

As we turn onto our street, we see Ashanti crouching by a flower pot in her front yard. A woman kneels beside her.

To my horror, Mom stops the car and gets out. Mom and Mrs. Smith, Ashanti's mom, hit it off. Mrs. Smith teaches at the university, too. Mr. Smith works for the alumni office. Ashanti and I might be in the same fifth-grade class!

"Ashanti just found her first colorful crab spider," Mrs. Smith says. "It's the fiftieth spider she's photographed for her collection."

Mom and Mrs. Smith keep talking. Ashanti photographs her spider. I trace circles in the dirt. Then Mrs. Smith asks Mom and me over for dinner. Mom agrees.

Yippee.

Ashanti rolls her eyes. She's not exactly thrilled, either.

Many crab spiders use camouflage to catch prey.

At six o'clock we're standing on the Smiths' front porch. Ashanti opens the door, and soon we sit down to dinner. The Smiths and Mom talk and laugh; Ashanti and I dig into our lasagna. Soon my plate is empty; so is Ashanti's.

She gives me a cautious look. "Want to see Anansi?" she asks quietly, so as not to interrupt the grownups.

I shrug. "I guess."

Ashanti smiles a little. "Come on."

We go into the family room. African artifacts cover three of the walls: masks, instruments, weavings, and paintings. A large bulletin board hangs on the fourth wall. About fifty photographs of spiders are mounted there. I take a deep breath and go over to the board.

I've got to admit, some of the spiders look pretty cool.

Ashanti points at a painting and says, "That's Anansi." I move closer to see a powerful-looking spider, standing upright, flexing six of its eight legs. The spider has a man's face . . . and eight eyes.

"Some legends say that Anansi created the sun, stars, and moon. Nice guy, huh?" Ashanti smiles. "He also could be tricky and greedy. In one story, he tries to keep all wisdom for himself."

Suddenly, Mrs. Smith calls from the kitchen, "Ashanti! Quick! You've got to see this!"

Ashanti turns and runs from the room with me at her heels.

Mr. and Mrs. Smith are peering at a baseboard. Ashanti presses close.

"Brown recluse!" Mrs. Smith whispers.

Ashanti gasps in excitement. She grabs her camera and adjusts the settings. Mom holds me back, although Mrs. Smith reassures her that the spider won't hurt you if you don't hurt the spider. Just don't brush up against it.

"Ashanti knows what to do, Mom," I say.

Ashanti glances at me, surprised, and smiles. Then she adjusts the zoom on her camera and snaps the picture. "Fifty-one!" she exclaims.

Later, after Mr. Smith has caught the venomous spider on a glue trap, Ashanti tells me that there's an interesting-looking web woven through my trampoline's net.

"I spotted it today on one of my safaris," she says, grinning. "I want to photograph it."

"Stop by tomorrow, if you want," I say.

"It'll be early in the morning. That's the best time."

"I'll probably be awake."

"Just don't be bouncing, OK? You might wreck it."

"I don't want to do that," I say. "I want to know which spiders live in *my* yard."

Boy, won't Billy be surprised. I'll be able to teach him a thing or two about spiders when he comes to visit!

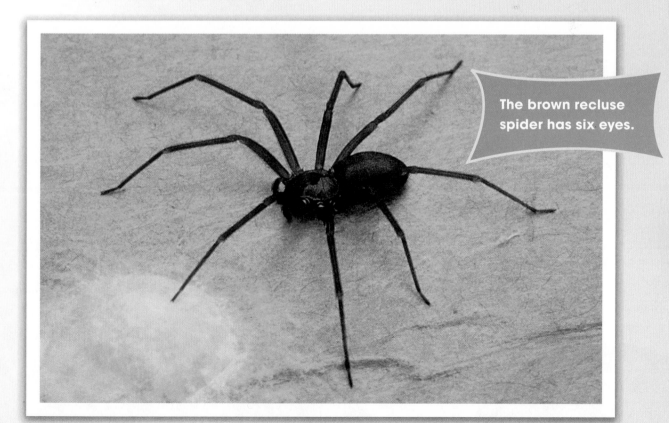

The brown recluse spider has six eyes.

WEB WISE

Part of what makes spiders fascinating is that they weave amazing webs. Here are a few facts to make you web wise.

Web Shots

Although it can be difficult to photograph a spider web, scientists and photographers know a few tricks to make it easier.

Some use cornstarch. The white powder coats the strands of the web and makes them easier to see. However, scientists know that this can sometimes damage the web. They always remove the spider before dusting the web.

Another method doesn't harm the web at all. Photographers spray a mist of water onto a web. Drops of water cling to the web's strands. Then sunshine turns an ordinary web into a sparkling jewel!

A Sticky Situation

Have you ever wondered why spiders don't get stuck in their own webs? The answer is simple: They know where they're going.

Most webs are made from two kinds of silk. An orb spider's web, for example, has long, straight strands that start at the middle and go out to the edges, like the spokes of a wheel. Then the web has a network of spiral strands in the center. The spiral strands are sticky, but the straight strands are not.

When an insect flies or crawls into the web, it gets stuck in the sticky strands. Then the spider hurries across the long, straight strands to enjoy its next meal!

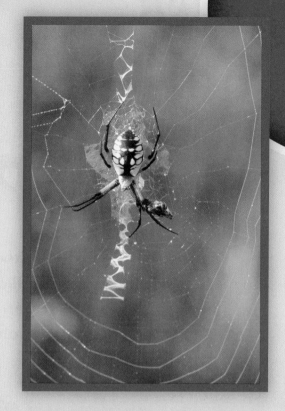

An orb spider's web is made of straight strands and spiral strands. The spiral strands are sticky.

Strange, but True!

More than 3,000 people visited a Texas state park during the 2007 Labor Day weekend. They didn't come to see parades or listen to speeches. They came to see a spider web!

It was no ordinary sight. The enormous web was draped over trees and shrubs along nearly 600 feet of a nature trail!

Scientists think millions of baby spiders, called *spiderlings*, built the web. The spiderlings may all have floated in on an air current and landed in the same area.

A few days later, heavy rain ruined the web.

The Spider

by Jack Prelutsky

The spider, sly and talented,
weaves silver webs of silken thread,
then waits for unobservant flies
… to whom she'll not apologize!

Spider Ropes

by James Berry

Alone in woods, I hunt
for pretty leaves dropped
and smooth stones like marbles.

I come back feeling
my face is well laced
with leaves and spiders' webs.

Design a Web!

If you were a spider, what kind of web would you weave? Look at the spider webs shown on this page, and then create your own design for a spider web.

Where would you make your web? What kinds of food would you hope to catch?

Write two or more sentences explaining how your web design would help you catch your lunch.

Story Scramble

Stories have a structure with a beginning, middle, and end. Events happen in an order that makes sense.

The story events below are scrambled. Put the letters in order so that the story makes sense. Then discuss how each event influences what happens next.

A. Despite the advice, Anansi threw down the pot, shouting, "The pot of wisdom is mine! I should know more than you!"

B. Anansi the spider had all the world's wisdom stored in a pot. The sky god Nyame had given it to him and told him to share it.

C. The pot broke. People found bits of wisdom scattered everywhere and took them home. That is why no one person today has all of the world's wisdom.

D. Greedy Anansi decided to hide the pot of wisdom at the top of a tree. Balancing the pot at the same time was tricky, though.

E. Anansi's young son told Anansi it would be easier to climb the tree with the pot tied to his back.

Two Tricksters

Compare and contrast Anansi's actions with those of Coyote in "The Sticky Coyote," Lesson 17, Student Book page 442.

Answers: B, D, E, A, C

Cool or

In "The Girl Who Loved Spiders," Luis thinks spiders are creepy until he meets Ashanti. Then he discovers that spiders are cool. Think about an animal that you really like or dislike. What is it about the animal that makes you feel the way you do? What details about the animal come to mind?

Write a poem about the animal you chose, or about an animal shown on these pages. Your poem may rhyme or use rhythm, like the one on pages 14 and 15.

Creepy?

Use descriptive details that create a vivid picture.

Think about the following:

- the animal's appearance
- the animal's movements
- how the animal sounds
- how the animal feels to the touch

The Frog in the Milk Pail

"I'm tired of sitting on this log," croaked a frog one sunny morning. So he jumped out of his pond and hopped off to explore.

Before long, the frog reached a fence. "How curious," he said. "I wonder if it tastes good." He flicked out his long tongue.

"Ugh!" he said.

The frog hopped along until he reached a brick path. "How curious," he said. "I wonder if it tastes good." He flicked out his long tongue.

"Ick!" he said.

The frog kept hopping until he saw a barn. "How curious," he said as he hopped up to the door. Just then he heard a loud *BZZZZ*.

"It's a fly!" cried the frog. "And after all this hopping, I'm hungry. "

The frog squeezed under the barn door. A big, fat fly was flying overhead. "Yum!" said the frog as he leaped into the air, but the fly was fast and flew away.

The frog, though, didn't land where he expected to. "How curious," said the frog. "I've landed in a pond with white water and shiny silver banks." Of course, it wasn't really a pond. It was a metal pail half-full of fresh milk.

The frog tried to climb out of the pail. But he just kept sliding back into the milk. He swam and splashed and kicked. He went faster and faster.

Then the frog noticed yellow globs floating in the milk. "How curious," he said. He went on swimming and splashing and kicking. He saw more yellow globs.

Before long there was a yellow hill in the middle of the pail. All that kicking and splashing and swimming had churned the milk into butter!

The frog climbed up the butter hill and jumped out of the pail. He hopped all the way home.

The moral of the story: Never give up.

The Science of Butter

Is making butter a chemical or a physical change? In a chemical change, a new chemical substance forms. Making butter is a physical change. The chemical makeup of the milk doesn't change. Churning simply makes drops of fat in the milk stick together to form butter.

SALAMANDER

AMPHIBIAN

Frogs, toads, salamanders, and newts are amphibians. The word *amphibian* means "double life" because these animals live part of their lives in water and part of their lives on land. An amphibian starts life in the water and then lives on land as an adult.

Amphibians lay their eggs in the water. These eggs do not have a hard shell. They are more like jelly. Young amphibians that hatch from the eggs look very different from adult amphibians. The young breathe with gills. They have tails that help them swim.

As young amphibians grow, their bodies change. They grow legs. Lungs develop and their gills disappear. These changes allow amphibians to live on land and breathe air with their lungs.

The skin of amphibians is not protected by hair, feathers, or scales like other animals. Their skin is permeable, which means they can absorb air and water through their skin.

Amphibians are found on all the continents except Antarctica. They are ancient animals that have been around for about 360 million years. However, their lives are being seriously threatened in today's world.

TREE FROG
Most amphibian species are frogs. This is a common tree frog.

ALERT!

Scientists know of approximately 6,000 different kinds of amphibians, but this number could change quickly. Scientists say that more than 120 amphibian species have already disappeared from the world. These kinds of amphibians are extinct, meaning that all members of the species have died.

Many different things are threatening the lives of amphibians, including habitat loss, pollution, introduced species, and a parasitic fungus. Scientists say that 2,000 to 3,000 of the amphibian species in the world are now threatened with extinction. It is the biggest extinction crisis in today's world.

NEWT
Most newts and salamanders are found in the cool forests of North America, Europe, and northern Asia.

This fire salamander lives in Hungary.

Habitat Loss and Pollution

Amphibians often live in swamps and ponds. But many of these swamps and ponds are being filled in to make way for roads, houses, and malls. Amphibians also live in rain forests that are being cut down or destroyed by fire. The loss of these habitats often leaves the amphibians nowhere to live.

Clean water is extremely important to amphibians. Adult amphibians need clean water to keep their skin moist. Adults lay their eggs in water, and young amphibians live completely in water.

Some ponds and creeks are close to farms. Chemical fertilizers are used on farms to grow better crops.

Pesticides are used to kill insects that destroy crops. However, when it rains, these chemicals are washed into the nearby ponds and creeks that lead to swamps and rivers.

Many frogs in these areas have been found with deformities, such as missing legs or extra legs. Deformed frogs like these have been found in 44 of the 50 United States. Some scientists believe that the chemical pollution in the water is absorbed by the soft eggs of amphibians and by their permeable skin. The chemical pollution affects the eggs and growth of the young, causing these deformities.

Blue poison dart frogs are endangered and found only in five forests of Suriname in South America.

Introduced Species and Fungus

Since the 1930s African clawed frogs have been shipped around the world by the thousands. These frogs are used in laboratory studies and for other purposes. Some exotic amphibians are shipped to other countries as pets or for food. Sometimes these amphibians escape or are released into their new habitat. In their new habitat they can cause problems.

The introduction of African clawed frogs into new areas has caused two major problems. African clawed frogs are more aggressive than many frogs, and they have been known to eat other frogs. But the bigger problem is that African clawed frogs carry a fungus called amphibian chytrid (KIT rid). This fungus does not hurt African clawed frogs, but it is deadly to many other kinds of amphibians.

● This cane toad lives in the Amazon jungle in Peru.

Scientists discovered this fungus about ten years ago. In the wild the fungus is unstoppable and untreatable. It can kill 80 percent of the amphibians in an area within months. Scientists suspect that dozens of frog species have gone extinct because of this fungus.

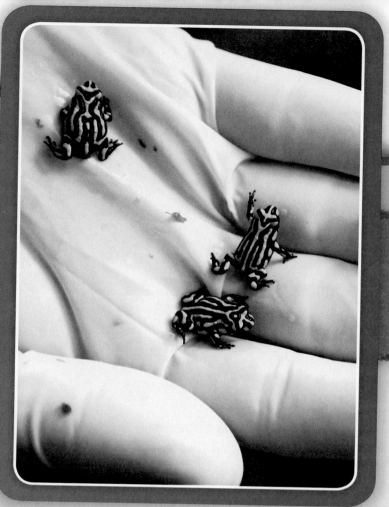

About 130 critically endangered Corroboree frogs are being protected and preserved at Taronga Zoo in Sydney, Australia. Only about 200 of these frogs are left in the wild.

Plans to Help

Scientists and conservation groups from around the world are putting plans together to help save amphibians. Much of their work focuses on the amphibian chytrid fungus because the disease it causes is the most serious and immediate threat.

Some scientists are researching how the disease spreads and why it kills only some individuals in one species, but kills all of another species. Other scientists are assessing the damage the disease has caused. The areas most affected so far include Central America, the Caribbean, Australia, and parts of Asia. However, scientists warn there is no continent or amphibian species that is safe.

Conservation groups that include many zoos are taking in many of the threatened amphibian species to protect and preserve them. In the future when the research scientists find ways to control the disease, the conservation groups will release these animals back into their natural habitat.

What We Can Do

Like scientists, you can do research and learn as much as you can about the problems facing frogs and other amphibians. You can search the Internet using search words, such as *threats to frogs and amphibians*, for more information. You can find maps and lists of the amphibian species in your area.

Amphibians live all over North America and in every state of the United States. The Appalachian range is home to many different species. Contact local nature preserves, zoos, or the office of environmental matters in your state to learn about volunteer opportunities.

You can also help by keeping local ponds and creeks clean. Although these small habitats may not seem as important as others, they are home to many creatures. We need to help preserve a future for them as well as for us.

A zookeeper at Taronga Zoo cares for Corroboree frog eggs (photo at right), tadpoles, and young frogs. Zoos all around the world are developing similar conservation programs to protect amphibian species from extinction.

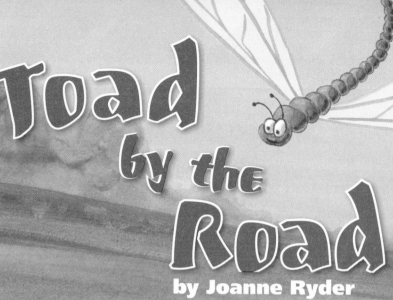

Toad by the Road

by Joanne Ryder

I'm only a toad
By the side of the road,
Watching the world go by.
Some hustle and hurry.
Some bustle and scurry.
Some wiggle, flicker, or fly.
They come and they go
On their way to and fro.
But I'd rather sit and sing.
It's a glorious day,
So I'm happy to stay
And savor the songs of spring.

THE POISON-DART FROGS

by Douglas Florian

Brown with oval orange spots.
Crimson mottled black with blots.
Neon green with blue-black bands.
Tangerine with lemon strands.
Banana yellow.
Ultramarine.
Almost any color seen.
And though their poison can tip a dart,
These frogs are Masters of Fine Art.

Match the MORAL

Three short frog fables follow, but the moral for each has gotten separated from its story. Match the moral to the fable it fits.

Morals

- Look before you leap.
- Choose your friends wisely.
- Beauty is in the eye of the beholder.

The Frogs and the Well

Two frogs lived in a small pond, but one hot summer it dried up. While looking for a new home, they came to a deep well.

"This looks like a cool, wet place to live. Let's dive in," said one frog.

"Not so fast, my friend. What if this well dries up like the pond? How would we get out?" replied the other frog.

Frog and Toad

A frog and a toad were sitting by a pond. Each thought himself handsome and the other ugly. A girl passed by and saw the two. "Yuck!" she cried as she ran away, disgusted by both.

The Mouse, the Frog, and the Hawk

A mouse and a frog were friends. One day the frog thought it would be fun to tie his leg to the mouse's. This was fine while they were in the meadow. Later, though, the frog hopped to the pond with the mouse. The poor mouse couldn't swim and drowned. A passing hawk snatched them both and flew to its nest. Still tied to the mouse, the frog also became the hawk's dinner.

Word Relationships

An *analogy* is a comparison of two sets of words. Each set of words has a similar relationship. Sometimes the words are *synonyms*, with similar meanings. Sometimes they are *antonyms*, with opposite meanings. The words in the example analogy have opposite meanings.

Example: *good* is to *bad* as *clean* is to *polluted*

Use the words in the box to complete the analogies.

ancient	extinct	habitat	major	preserve

1. alive is to _____ as right is to wrong

2. guard is to protect as save is to _____

3. home is to neighborhood as pond is to _____

4. old is to _____ as new is to current

5. _____ is to minor as large is to little

Hint:

Think about the relationship of the words to help you pick the right answer.

SAVE the FROGS!

and other amphibians

In "Amphibian Alert!" you learned about some of the problems that amphibians are facing in the world today. Create a board game about amphibians that are losing their home for one of the reasons given in the article. Have the amphibians look for a new home.

After you have drawn up the plan for your board game, write a set of instructions for how to play the game.

START

Pond is too small.

Lose one turn.

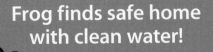

Frog finds safe home with clean water!

FINISH

- Start with a sentence that states what the instructions are for.
- List all necessary materials.
- List each step in the game. Make sure the steps are in the right order.
- Tell how the game is won.

Remember to write each step in your instructions as a complete sentence.

Pond is polluted by chemicals.

Go back 3 spaces.

Deadly fungus in the area.

Return to start.

African clawed frogs live here.

Go back 2 spaces.

Museums
Worlds of Wonder

Museums are wonderful places.

That doesn't just mean "terrific places." It means places that fill you with wonder—that surprise and amaze you. It also means places that *make* you wonder—about the world, about nature, about history, about people.

How do museums do that? No two museums do it in the same way. There are art museums, science museums, historical museums, and nature museums. There are museums that focus on a single subject, like music boxes or postage stamps, and there are museums that seem to go in dozens of different directions at once.

Here is a brief tour of five museums that are very different from each other. But all of them are full of wonders.

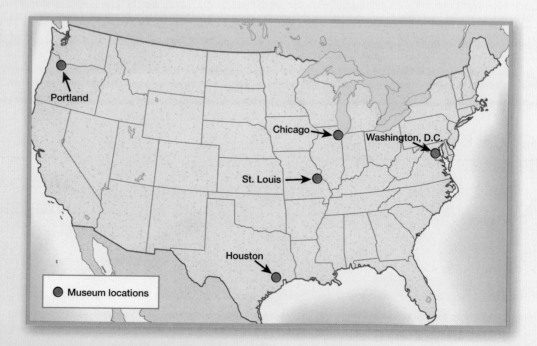

Portland

Chicago

Washington, D.C.

St. Louis

Houston

● Museum locations

City Museum of
St. Louis, Missouri

The first thing you should know about the City Museum of St. Louis is that it is located in an old shoe factory. It's no surprise, then, that this museum believes in preserving the past and recycling—making something new out of something old. There's also an amazing playground called MonstroCity that's made mostly of recycled materials from the city of St. Louis, including giant metal springs, a castle turret, and the body of a jet plane.

Artist Bob Cassilly designed the City Museum as a huge work of art. Take the Enchanted Caves. Where shoes once moved on conveyor belts through tunnels, children now run into petrified dragons and climb spiral staircases. In Art City, you can watch glass blowers at work, and make your own work of art, too. Then there's the museum *inside* the museum. It's called The Museum of Mirth, Mystery, and Mayhem and it's like an old-fashioned carnival. Finally, let's not forget the World Aquarium, home to more than 10,000 sea creatures, from stingrays to seahorses.

National Air and Space Museum
in Washington, DC

Are you interested in space and flight? Have you ever wondered where the Wright Brothers' original airplane is? If so, then the National Air and Space Museum is the place for you. It has the largest collection of aircraft and spacecraft in the world.

Begin with the Milestones of Flight Exhibit. You'll see the *Spirit of St. Louis*, the first plane to be flown nonstop across the Atlantic Ocean by a solo pilot. Want some faster fliers? Check out the *Airacomet*, the first American jet, and the X-15, which flew six times the speed of sound! Upstairs you'll find the airplane that made it all possible: the *Flyer*, which Orville and Wilbur Wright first flew in 1903.

Next, let your imagination soar into space. This museum is home to *Sputnik I*, the first satellite to successfully orbit Earth, and the *Apollo 11* command module, which carried the first men to the moon. Here also are replicas of spacecraft that have flown to Mars, Venus, and Jupiter.

The Albert Einstein Planetarium lets you feel what it might be like to zoom through the galaxy. The Ride Simulator takes you on a virtual space walk. Finally, there is a real moon rock you can touch that the *Apollo 17* astronauts brought back.

Field Museum
in Chicago, Illinois

You could spend days exploring the Field Museum in the city of Chicago. The museum contains more than twenty million items, including mummies, meteorites, and mammals. With so much to see, you might not have time to meet Sue. That would be a mistake.

Sue is the largest *Tyrannosaurus rex* skeleton ever found, as well as the most complete. Sue is forty-two feet long with more than two hundred bones—real bones, not plaster ones. All except for Sue's second skull. It's a case of two heads being better than one.

Sue's five-foot-long skull was so big and heavy that the museum staff had to put it in a glass case by itself. They made a lighter model for the skeleton on display. You can put your nose just inches from Sue's real skull—if you dare. You also can handle models of some of Sue's bones, including a huge tooth and a rib. By the way, Sue was named after Sue Hendrickson, the woman who found "her" in South Dakota. No one really knows if Sue is male or female.

World Forestry Center and Discovery Museum
in Portland, Oregon

A museum that's about trees? The World Forestry Center's Discovery Museum will make you appreciate forests more than ever before—including forests around the world.

On the first floor of the museum, you can explore forests that grow in the Pacific Northwest. You can discover what lives under the forest and then take a ride to explore the tree-tops. On another ride you can learn how smokejumpers fight forest fires. The museum shows the many things that forests provide, such as wood, water, habitat, and clean air.

On the second floor, a giant wall map tells about different types of forests worldwide. Then you can see for yourself. Take a train ride to the forests of Siberia and a boat ride to a forest lake in China. Ride a jeep to visit forest animals in South Africa. Look down on the canopy of Brazil's Amazon rainforest.

American Cowboy Museum
at Taylor-Stevenson Ranch
near Houston, Texas

Many museums are important for changing old ideas people may have. Through hands-on exhibits, talks, and even horseback riding, the American Cowboy Museum gives the true history of a popular legend. There is a lot we can learn about the American cowboy. For example, did you know that as many as one-third of all cowboys were African Americans? Many cowboys were Native Americans, and the first cowboys, or *vaqueros*, were from Mexico. And of course, "cowboys" also included women.

The museum is part of the Taylor-Stevenson Ranch, which is 150 years old. It has been owned by generations of an African American family. About fifty years ago, the family started the museum to honor the part Native Americans, African Americans, Hispanics, and women played in settling the West. The founders, Mollie Stevenson, Jr. and her mother, Mollie Stevenson, Sr. are also the first living African Americans in the National Cowgirl Hall of Fame.

MAKING THE MOST FROM TRASH

Trash is a huge problem. We make mountains of it every day. But there are three things we can do to help fix the problem. First, we can REDUCE what we use. Second, we can REUSE things, rather than just throw them away. Third, we can RECYCLE. Often one thing can be recycled into something entirely different.

Flakes to Fleece

Did you know that plastic bottles can have a second life as a fleece jacket? Here's how. The plastic bottles are cleaned and chopped into flakes. Later, the flakes are melted down and squeezed into threads. Like wool, the threads are spun into yarn and woven into fleece. The fleece can be sewn into a jacket, hat, or a warm pair of socks. It takes about twenty-five two-liter plastic soda bottles to make a jacket.

Tires to Playgrounds

Where do all the old tires go? The lucky ones are recycled into firm but bouncy playground surfaces. Maybe you have felt how comfortable it is to walk in a rubber-soled shoe. Well, someone had the idea to chop up old tires and mold the rubber pieces into a squishy rubber surface for playgrounds. It saves children from being hurt, it recycles rubber, and it's fun to play on! So go ahead and bounce!

Milk Jugs to Chairs

Have you ever noticed the number two inside a triangle on the bottom of a milk jug? That symbol means the milk jug could have another life as a chair. Type two plastic, also called HDPE, gets recycled into all kinds of sturdy furniture. It looks like painted wood, but it will last longer. You can even buy trash cans made from recycled plastic. How fitting is that?

Dinosaur Bone

by Alice Schertle

Dinosaur bone
alone, alone;
keeping a secret
old as stone

deep in the mud
asleep in the mud
tell me, tell me,
dinosaur bone

What was the world
when the seas were new
and ferns unfurled
and strange winds blew?

Were the mountains fire?
Were the rivers ice?
Was it mud and mire?
Was it paradise?

How did it smell,
your earth, your sky?
How did you live?
How did you die?

How long have you lain
alone, alone?
Tell me, tell me,
dinosaur bone.

Museum Farewell

by Rebecca Kai Dotlich

Lights out.
Doors close
on the cool quiet
of museum spaces;
echoing hallways,
        locked cases—

room upon room
all silent now.

Amazing how
    museums hold
        an ancient secret,
            a whispered spell.

Close these doors.

Lights out.

        Farewell.

Activity Central

Come to the MUSEUM!

Museums often advertise to tell people about new or special exhibits. Create an ad for a real or imaginary museum. You might design your ad as a jingle to sing on the radio, a billboard, or a poster. Include in your ad three facts about the museum a visitor would need to know. Your ad might tell where the museum is located, when it's open, and what its special exhibits are. You could also include quotes from people who have visited the museum. For example, "Ed Crowe" might say: "I think this is the best museum I've ever been to!"

Meet Sue, the largest and most complete T-rex skeleton ever found!

"It's thrilling!" exclaims Lisa

"Awesome" Joe agrees

Sue is 42 feet long with more than 200 real bones. Sue resides at the Field Museum in Chicago.

Impossible? NOT!

The poem below is about exploring with words. However, some of its words are missing! The words in the box have the prefixes *im-* and *in-*. On another sheet of paper, use each word to fill in the blanks. Check the spelling of the prefix and base word that make up each word.

inexpensive	injustice	independence
incredible	immeasurable	

Climb to the top of Mount Everest
And take in the _____ view.
Explore the sea's _____ depths
With Captain Nemo and his daring crew.

March with Martin Luther King Jr.
to protest _____ in our nation.
Listen to Thomas Jefferson speak
Of _____ and unfair taxation.

Impossible! Improbable! Is that what you say?
Well, that's incorrect! You can do it today.

Exploring can be _____.
It doesn't have to cost you a dime.
All you need are two simple things:
An interesting book and some time!

Answers: incredible, immeasurable, injustice, independence, inexpensive

EXPRESS YOURSELF!

Is your school or community doing what it can to recycle its trash? Do you see ways that recycling could be improved? Express your opinion, or yours and a partner's, in a letter to a leader of your school or community.

Tell what's working or, if necessary, include your own ideas to improve recycling efforts. For example, maybe each classroom could have a bin for recycling paper. Coming up with suggestions helps support your opinion.

WRITING TIPS

- Begin your letter by giving an example of the problem.

- State your opinion of the situation.

- Be positive about how the problem could be handled.

- Suggest possible solutions and offer to help.

SAVE TIMBER WOODS!

CAST OF CHARACTERS

**Narrator • Lucas • Laura
Gina • Hector**

Scene I

Setting: The kitchen in Gina's home on the edge of the woods

Narrator: Laura, Gina, Hector, and Lucas are researching a current event for school. Gina is searching on a laptop. The others are looking through newspapers.

Lucas: What if we do our report on gas prices?

Laura: Boring!

(Suddenly, Gina sees a deer outside in the yard. She jumps up from her chair and dashes to the kitchen door, shouting.)

Gina: Get out of there! Scram!

(Grabbing a broom, Gina charges out the door, waving the broom and yelling as the deer runs away.)

Laura: Why did you yell at that deer, Gina? It was so cute.

Gina *(Outraged)*: Cute? Maybe, if you only see them once in a while; but they've started to show up in our yard every day. They are eating the tree we planted when my little sister was born!

Narrator: Gina points at a small tree on the lawn. Its branches are nearly bare.

Gina *(Calming down)*: Those deer and our neighborhood don't go together.

Hector: We have deer at my house, too. My dad says it's because the deer have no place to go. People are building homes where the deer used to live. Now they have to find food somewhere else.

Gina *(In an annoyed voice)*: Well, not in my backyard.

Lucas: The poor deer lost their homes, Gina.

Gina: Well, my poor family is losing our favorite tree.

Hector *(Holding up the newspaper he's been looking through, excitedly)*: Hey! Listen to this! Here's an article that says the deer problem is going to get worse. Land developers plan to cut down Timber Woods, by the school. Our town government has been renting the woods from a private owner. Now the owner plans to sell it to a developer who plans to build one hundred townhouses.

Laura: Timber Woods? That's where we do fieldwork for science class. That's where we camp and have picnics.

Lucas: What about the animals who live there? More animals will get kicked out of their homes.

Gina: More yards will be ruined by deer!

Hector: Well, at least we found a current event to report on.

Laura: I wish we could stop them from cutting down Timber Woods.

Hector: Maybe it's not too late. The paper says that people can talk about the development plan at next week's town council meeting. Let's ask our parents if we can go. Right now, let's find more information to put into our current events report.

Gina: Let's get all the facts. That way we'll have a good report for class and good ideas for the council meeting.

Lucas: Maybe our friends will come to the meeting.

Narrator: The group presents its current events report and the whole class gets excited. The class decides to ask the town's leaders to buy Timber Woods and preserve the land for both animals and people.

Scene II

Setting: The next day, in the dining room of Gina's home

Narrator: The four friends are making signs for the meeting. Gina and Lucas are working on a large sign.

Laura: What is your sign going to say?

Gina and Lucas: "Save Timber Woods."

Lucas: "Save the animals from us . . . "

Gina: ". . . and save our yards from the animals!"

Hector: It's about the woods, too. Remember that book we read about the water cycle? It said that natural areas, such as woods, help absorb water and prevent flooding when heavy rains fall or snow melts. But how can I put that on a sign?

Laura: How about: "Woods and water—important partners. Ask me why."

Hector: Good idea! Then I can talk about it when I give our statement.

Gina: It's cool that the town council said you could present a statement from us, Hector. But how will the town ever get enough money to buy the woods? I also heard my mom talking about how much money the city will get from new taxpayers who move into the new houses.

Lucas: But the problems caused by cutting the woods will cost money. We have to help them see that.

Hector *(Pointing at Lucas)*: You're right. Instead of ignoring the issue of money, we should show that we understand it. Let's do some more research so we know the facts. And how about this for a sign: "Saving Timber Woods saves dollars and makes sense."

Laura: At least the town will know how we feel.

Scene III

Setting: A meeting room with rows of folding chairs, inside the town hall

Hector: I'm nervous.

Laura: You're going to be great, Hector. Look, I think that's the developer!

Hector: Maybe he could tear down those old Smithfield warehouses and build homes there. Nobody has used those buildings for a long time.

Lucas: Good idea. *(Turning around)* I think the meeting's about to start.

Narrator: The town council members soon introduce the main topic: the sale of Timber Woods. People take turns talking about the plan to build townhouses. Finally, it's Hector's turn to speak. The audience listens closely as he explains why the woods are so important, and what the students want the council to do.

Hector *(In a firm voice)*: So, we ask the adults in town to join us in finding a way to turn Timber Woods into protected parkland.
(He sits down as many people applaud.)

Narrator: After more debate, the council decides to delay the sale of Timber Woods for three months. During that time, the town will try to raise enough money to buy the woods. After the meeting, the students get together.

Gina *(In an excited voice)*: They listened to us after all.

Laura: Now we have to help find ways to raise money.

Lucas: How about a car wash?

Hector: That's a good idea, but we'll need to do more than that.

Laura: Let's meet tomorrow.

Gina: Let's involve the whole class. Everyone will benefit if we can save Timber Woods, so we should all work together.

Reading the Play
With a partner, describe the structural features of the play—the scenes, dialogue, and stage directions—and discuss how they helped you follow the events.

FOLLOWING MUIR:

A Persuasive Essay

John Muir was a protector of nature. He set an example that each of us can follow to protect the natural areas around us.

The first way we can follow Muir's example is to discover our local natural areas. Muir was a great walker. He once walked one thousand miles from Indiana to Florida. He also took a 250-mile walk from San Francisco, California, to the Yosemite (yoh SEH mih tee) Valley, in the heart of the Sierra Nevada Mountains.

Another way to follow Muir is to learn about nature. Muir loved to explore the outdoors. He learned everything he could about rocks, plants, and animals. From his exploring, he came to realize that the wilderness, places where people do not live or build, is an important gift. Muir decided that his life's goal was to protect this gift.

Muir's greatest example for us is his work to protect nature. He shared its beauty by writing books. He climbed Yosemite's towering peaks and described them as "clothed in light." In winter, he delighted in its "pearl-gray belt of snow." However, he also saw sheep eating Yosemite's plants and people chopping down its trees for wood. Muir gave talks and wrote books about these dangers. President Theodore Roosevelt was so impressed after hearing Muir that he visited Yosemite. In 1890, Roosevelt signed a bill making Yosemite a national park. This meant that the U.S. government would take care of it.

We can find our own pieces of nature to explore, learn about, and protect. We can write to our local newspapers about nature's beauty and tell people how to help care for it. We can all follow in John Muir's footsteps.

John Muir Timeline

1838 ● Born in Scotland

1849 ● Family moves to the United States

1867 ● Walks from Indiana to Florida

1868 ● Walks from San Francisco to Yosemite Valley

1890 ● Helps Yosemite become a national park

1892 ● Forms the Sierra Club

1903 ● Camps with President Theodore Roosevelt in Yosemite

1912 ● Travels to South America and Africa

1914 ● Dies of pneumonia on December 24

Analyzing the Essay

On a sheet of paper, list details the author used that you think helped persuade the reader. Explain to a partner why you think so.

The Comb of Trees
A Secret Sign Along the Way

By Claudia Lewis

Riding to Rock Creek
for our picnics
we swing around
a certain curve
and then I see it—

Standing high
on a mountain ridge
a little row
of firs, with trunks
tall and bare,
lined up one by one—
a comb
against the sky.

As we draw near
each time
I wonder—

it…?
    Is it…?

        Then we turn—

        Yes! It's there!

No storm
has wrecked my comb,
no lumberjack
has chopped it down—

All's well
still
(a while?)
up there.

Enjoy the Earth

Yoruba, Africa

Enjoy the earth gently
Enjoy the earth gently
For if the earth is spoiled
It cannot be repaired
Enjoy the earth gently

The Impact of Life's Events

Your timeline should end with an arrow to show that the line will continue.

1st

Spelling Bee

Born

A timeline of a person's life often includes events that impact or shape the person. Look back at the essay about John Muir. The timeline shows important events that shaped who he was. It also shows the dates for when he was born and when he died.

Create a timeline about your life. Include the year of your birth and four important events in your life.

Write About It Choose one event from your timeline. Write a paragraph telling about the event and why it was important.

Your timeline begins with a point and gives the date you were born.

1st

Say It with a Sign

Tear down warehouses— NOT WOODS!

Preserve our Picnic Place!

People use signs to show their feelings in a public place, as the students do in "Save Timber Woods!" The students want the town council to know how they feel about the proposed sale of Timber Woods to a developer. So they make signs that the people going to the meeting will see.

Make a sign that the students in the story could use to save Timber Woods. Or make a sign about a local habitat you want to save. Try to make your message clear in as few words as possible.

Try to See

In "Save Timber Woods!" the friends persuade a town to protect a threatened woodland habitat. The photos on these pages show four common woodland animals. Choose one, or a different animal whose habitat might be in danger. Write a persuasive essay explaining why it is important to protect the animal's home. Use "Following Muir: A Persuasive Essay" as a model for writing your essay.

Be sure to include the following:
- an introductory paragraph that states the point you will be making
- at least three reasons or examples that support that point
- one paragraph for each reason or example
- a concluding paragraph that restates the point you have made

It My Way!

MYSTERY

Once a week, Ms. Cabrera's science class spent an afternoon outside, working in teams to observe different habitats. Adrian, Mara, and Nicole were assigned pond patrol. Adrian wondered if his team had gotten the best assignment because of his extra-sharp eyes.

Reed's Pond lay at the end of a shady, sloping path. Pine trees towered overhead. Bushes and moss-covered rocks rimmed the shore. Adrian had been the first one in class to spot the turtle at the pond—even though its brown shell and wrinkled skin blended in perfectly with its surroundings.

"Here, Brownie . . . here, Brownie," Adrian whispered as he approached the water's edge. But today, the turtle that peeked from the water looked different. Instead of a little brown face, this one had streaks of red near each eye.

"Brownie? Are you wearing makeup?" From what Adrian could see, the turtle's shell looked different, too. Today it was green with yellow stripes.

The girls hurried over. When the turtle came up for another breath, Nicole noticed the changes, too.

"That's not Brownie. That's a different kind of turtle," she said. "Its name should be Red Dot."

"Maybe Brownie's somewhere else," said Mara.

They continued their pond patrol, but Adrian had a strange feeling that something wasn't right. Sure enough, his hunch was correct.

"Look!" Mara shouted. She was pointing at a bird's nest or what used to be a bird's nest.

Just last week they had written about the nest in their logs. It was a carefully made cup of sticks nestled in a low-hanging branch. There had been three brown eggs in it. Now the branch was broken. The bowl was squashed into a messy ball.

"Where are the eggs?" asked Nicole.

Adrian crouched under the branch, which jutted out over some rocks at the water's edge. He saw one egg smashed into a crevice between two rocks. He couldn't see any sign of the other two eggs.

"Do you think an animal did this to the nest?" Nicole wondered.

"An animal couldn't have turned Brownie into Red Dot," said Adrian.

"And an animal wouldn't have left this," said Mara. She held up a shopping bag that she had found. "There's lettuce in it. Maybe it's a clue."

"A clue to what?" asked Nicole.

Ms. Cabrera's whistle blew. It was time to go back to class.

"We need to do some more investigating," said Mara. "Let's meet here Saturday, when we have more time."

The weather on Saturday was sunny and warm, but no one else was at the pond. Nicole, Mara, and Adrian scanned the area. Adrian soon found the new turtle. It sat basking on a rock at the edge of the water. When it saw the three children, it quickly slid into the water. The ripples spread and soon faded. Then Adrian, Mara, and Nicole went to investigate the bird's nest. The clump of sticks remained, but there were no new clues about what had destroyed the nest or where the two eggs had gone.

Many turtles like to bask, or warm themselves, in the sun.

"This is the case of the missing turtle and eggs," Mara said.

"Shh," whispered Adrian. He could hear leaves crunching on the path. "Someone's coming. Hide!"

The three crouched in the bushes. Through the leaves, they could see a teenaged boy wearing a blue backpack. At the edge of the pond, the boy swung it from his shoulder and knelt down. Adrian held his breath. He could hear his heart beating. Had the boy noticed them?

The boy seemed to think he was alone, however. He reached into his backpack and pulled out a turtle whose shell was as big as a plate. It was bright green, with yellow and green markings on the belly. Suddenly the turtle's head shot out of the shell and snapped at the boy's wrist. The boy dropped the turtle into the pond. The splash rang out as loud as a slap. Adrian saw the red dashes on the turtle's face.

The boy darted back up the path and quickly vanished.

"So that's where Red Dot came from," whispered Nicole.

"Red Dot was already here on Thursday, though," said Adrian. "This is the same kind of turtle, but it's not the *same* turtle. Also, what about Brownie? Where's he?"

"We've got to talk to that boy," said Mara. "Come on." Adrian wasn't sure it was a good idea, but Mara was already running up the path. He and Nicole followed.

"Excuse me!" Mara called out when she reached the field. The boy turned to look but kept striding toward his bike.

"I just want to ask you about the turtle," Mara said.

"I don't know what you're talking about," the boy said. "I don't know anything about turtles." He got on his bike.

"We just saw you drop one into the pond!" Mara shouted. It didn't matter. The boy pedaled off without looking back.

"Something fishy is going on," Nicole said.

"Something turtle-y, you mean," replied Adrian.

"I think it's time for a little research," said Mara.

Red-eared sliders are popular pets.

On Monday, they told Ms. Cabrera what they had seen. During science, she gave them time to research on the computer. Mara typed the words *red dot turtle* into the search engine. Links for turtleneck sweaters, Turtle Island, and a video game came up.

"This won't help," said Nicole.

"Don't give up yet," said Mara. She typed in *red turtle*. That was better. Lots of listings appeared for a turtle called a red-eared slider. The first thing Mara did was to click on the images.

"That's it!" said Adrian, as a photo appeared. "That's Red Dot, all right."

With a few more mouse-clicks, the students learned that the turtles were common pets. They also learned that the red-eared slider's natural habitat was east of the Rocky Mountains. "So what is one doing in a pond in California?" asked Nicole.

Mara typed *red-eared slider in California* into the search engine.

Among the listings of turtles for sale and questions about pet turtles, they saw an article from a California paper. The three of them read silently.

The article told about people dumping their pet turtles into local waters and the problems that occurred as a result. "Mystery solved!" said Mara.

"Ms. Cabrera!" they called.

"It looks like the pond patrol might have uncovered some illegal activity," Ms. Cabrera said when they told her what they had learned. "Let's report it to the water district."

That Thursday, Ms. Cabrera's class had a special observation day at the pond. Mr. Roberts, an officer from the water district, was with them. He had brought nets for capturing the red-eared sliders. Adrian spotted the first one, basking near the ruined bird's nest. Working together, the class helped Mr. Roberts catch two more.

"We'll take them to a turtle sanctuary," Mr. Roberts explained. "It's a place where they keep the turtles safe until someone can adopt them."

While Mr. Roberts talked, Adrian was looking for his old friend.

"Brownie!" said Adrian when he saw the head peek up. "Look, Mr. Roberts. That's the turtle I'm used to seeing."

"That's a western pond turtle. It's just the kind of turtle we want to see around here."

"I never knew what kind he was. I just knew I liked him," said Adrian. *Western pond turtle*, he wrote in his log.

Western pond turtles live in California, Oregon, and Washington.

"We got the sliders out just in time. Red-eared sliders are big. They eat the same things as the western pond turtles, and the western pond turtles can't compete," said Mr. Roberts.

"What about the bird eggs?" asked Nicole. "Did the turtles have anything to do with those?"

"Probably, but we can't be sure," said Mr. Roberts. "Red-eared sliders like to bask on nests. They can squash the nests and crush the eggs."

"That's another reason why people shouldn't leave their pets here," said Ms. Cabrera. She was posting a sign on a tree. DON'T DUMP YOUR PETS. BRING PET TURTLES TO VALLEY TURTLE SANCTUARY.

"Thanks for helping us save the native species," Mr. Roberts told the class. "I have something for Adrian, Mara, and Nicole." He handed them each an envelope and a patch that said *Water District* with a picture of a river.

"The water district invites you to be its first junior officers," Mr. Roberts said. "We'd also like to offer each of you a scholarship to ecology camp this summer. You can talk it over with your parents."

"Thanks!" said Adrian. He'd never thought his sharp eyes would actually help wildlife survive.

A Big

A Dangerous Predator

Pythons come from Asia and Africa and are among the longest snakes in the world. They can grow to be more than twenty feet long—longer than a large pickup truck. Their bodies can be as thick as a telephone pole. Pythons' mouths can stretch so wide they can swallow prey as large as deer and alligators.

Surprisingly, baby pythons are popular pets in this country. But pythons grow quickly. In a year, a tiny baby can become an eight-foot long snake. As time passes, it grows even bigger. Many owners have trouble caring for such large, dangerous animals. Sometimes, they take their snake and leave it in the wild.

In most areas of the United States, pythons wouldn't have enough warmth, water, or space to survive. Places like southern Florida, though, have a perfect climate for pythons. Because of this, pythons are causing serious trouble in Florida's Everglades National Park.

Adult pythons can weigh up to 200 pounds.

Python Problem

Can the Problem Be Solved?

Scientists are not sure how many pythons are in the Everglades, but they estimate that there are thousands. The big snakes eat the animals that make their natural home in the park. Some of these animals are endangered, such as the Key Largo cotton mouse and the white ibis, a water bird. Pythons have also eaten the pets of people who live in the area.

Park officials are trying to solve this big problem. They are using different methods to capture pythons. They have tried using radio transmitters to lure snakes to places where they can be caught. And they have even trained a dog to help. "Python Pete" is a beagle that can smell pythons and alert humans to their presence.

Python Pete is doing a good job. But people have to learn not to buy exotic pets they cannot take care of. Teaching people to think through their pet-buying decisions is also part of the fight against the python.

Python Pete has been trained to pick up the scent of pythons.

Naming the Turtle

by Patricia Hubbell

Slowpod,
Weightlifter,
Housemover,
Homelover.

Seaflipper,
Rainstopper,
Pond-land-
and-stream-dweller.

Platepacker,
Boneback,
Hardshell
and Softhat.

Clicktoe
and Stare-eye,
Budhead
and Stemneck.

Nob-bob and
Lookslow,
Spotback
and Ridgetop.

Plod-plod
and Plopplop,

Logloving
Rockstone.

Greater Flamingo

by Tony Johnston

Pale as the pink lip
of a shell, it drinks from its
cool green reflection

YOU BE THE DETECTIVE

Read about the events below. From the set of clues, draw a conclusion about what happened.

The Missing Clown Fish

The Ringling School's Grade 4 class has a saltwater aquarium. It contains an eel and three large angelfish. On Monday, a family donates two colorful clown fish. On Tuesday morning, Roy Gee, "the class clown," reports one clown fish missing. What happened?

CLUES

- The school's night janitor says the clown fish looked fine at 7:00 p.m.
- Roy Gee says he'll be the other clown fish's friend.
- The three large angelfish are still in the aquarium and look no different.
- The eel does not eat its regular frozen shrimp on Tuesday morning.
- A book about the care of eels is unopened. In fact, it's covered with a layer of dust.

The eel ate the clown fish. Because the class hadn't read the eel book, they didn't realize the danger. Angelfish are big enough to avoid being eaten by the eel.

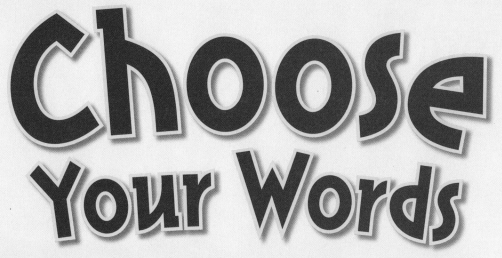

Choose Your Words

Using just the right word can help a reader understand exactly how something looks, sounds, acts, or feels. The following Found Pet announcement is on a bulletin board. You finish it. On a piece of paper, write a list of words and phrases to fill in the blanks. Make sure they describe the pet and other details exactly.

Have you lost a _____ snake?

I found a snake in _____. The snake looks _____. When I try to hold it, the snake _____. I think it is feeling _____. I think it may be a python, because it _____. The only sound it makes is _____. I'm keeping the snake in _____. Hurry!

Found Snake

House For Rent

Yard Sale

24 Oak St.

Pets Need You!

Having a pet can be hard work. Sometimes pet owners can't take care of their pets any longer but don't know what to do with them. You've read about some problems this causes.

Search on the Internet for information about how to care for pets properly. Then write an essay of at least three paragraphs that an animal shelter employee might hand out to someone thinking about caring for a pet.

ANIMAL SHELTER

Do I have time to care for a pet?

Here are some tips:

🐾 Start with an introduction to possible pet owners. Encourage them to think about whether owning a pet is right for them. End the essay with a conclusion that sums up your ideas.

🐾 Give examples of the responsibilities of pet ownership (food, water, shelter, exercise).

🐾 Give examples of problems that can be caused when people abandon their pets (problems for the pet, for the environment, and for animal shelters).

🐾 Use a variety of sentence types and clear transitions between paragraphs.

Credits

Photo Credits

KEY: (t) top, (b) bottom, (l) left, (r) right, (c) center, (bg) background, (fg) foreground, (i) inset

Cover (cl) Peter Hvizdak/The Image Work; (bg) Chad Ehlers/Alamy; (bl) Juniors Bildarchiv/photolibrary; RA3 (t) Richard T. Nowitz/Corbis; (b) Corbis; RA14 (l) PhotoDisc/Getty Images; (r) Thomas Northcut/Getty Images; RA16 (l) Getty Images/ PhotoDisc /Siede Preis; (bc) Getty Images/PhotoDisc / Siede Preis; RA17 (bl) Getty Images/PhotoDisc / Siede Preis; (r) Getty Images/PhotoDisc / Siede Preis; (b) Harcourt School Publishers; RA18 (l) Corbis; RA30 (bg) Getty Images/PhotoDisc; RA31 (cr) Corbis; RA32 (bl) Arco Images GmbH / Alamy; RA33 (bg) Mark Karrass/Corbis; RA34 (bg) Mark Karrass/Corbis; RA35 (tr) Robb Kendrick; RA36 (bg) Geoff Renner; RA37 (br) Gerald & Buff Corsi/Visuals Unlimited, Inc.; (t) Peter Barritt / Alamy; RA38 (bg) Corbis; RA39 (bc) AFP/Getty Images; RA42 (bg) Gerald Kooyman/ Corbis; RA43 (bc) PhotoDisc/Getty Images; RA65 (b) Brand X Pictures / Getty Images; RA66 (t) Richard T. Nowitz/ Corbis; RA69 (bg) Goodshoot/Jupiterimages/Getty Images; RA71 (bg) Radius Images / Alamy; RA72 (inset) Dennis Van Tine ./Retna Ltd./Corbis; (inset) Hisham Ibrahim/Photodisc/Getty Images; (bg) Don Farrall/Photodisc/Getty Images; RA75 (bg) Corbis; Title Page (cr) Chad Ehlers/Alamy; (b) Tina Manley/Alamy; 1 (br) Getty Images/PhotoDisc; 2 (tl) Angelo Cavalli/AGE Fotostock; 2 (cl) Angela Hampton Picture Library/Alamy; 3 (cr) Martin Harvey/Getty Images; (tr) Tony Fagan/Alamy; 7 (bc) Jason Edwards/National Geographic Image Collection; 8 (b) SuperStock; 11 (b) David M. Dennis/Oxford Scientific/photolibrary; 12 (bl) Johnny Greig/Alamy; 13 (bl) Tom Pennington/Newscom; (tr) Georgette Douwma/Getty Images; 16 (b) Chad Ehlers/Alamy; (bc) Mauritius/SuperStock; 18 (br) Getty Images/PhotoDisc; 19 (cr) Getty Images/PhotoDisc; (bl) Getty Images/PhotoDisc; 22 (bg) Siede Preis/Getty Images; (t) Angelo Cavalli/AGE Fotostock; (bl) Siede Preis/Getty Images; (br) Siede Preis/Getty Images; 23 (b) Brand X Pictures/AGE Fotostock; (t) Klaus Honal/AGE Fotostock; 24 (bg) Siede Preis/Getty Images; (bl) Siede Preis/Getty Images; (t) Paul Oomen/Getty Images; 25 (b) George Grall /Getty Images; (br) Siede Preis/Getty Images; (t) Stan Osolinski/Corbis; 26 (t) Ian Waldie/Getty Images; (bl) Siede Preis/Getty Images; (bg) Siede Preis/Getty Images; 27 (r) Ian Waldie/Getty Images; (l) Ian Waldie/ Getty Images; 30 (cr) Stockbyte/Getty Images; (b) Stockbyte/Getty Images; (bl) Stockbyte/Getty Images; (c) Stockbyte/ Getty Images; 31 MedioImages/Corbis; 35 (t) AP Photo/James A. Finley; 36 (b) William S. Kuta/Alamy; 37 (t) Stephen McBrady/PhotoEdit; 38 (t) Andre Jenny/Alamy; 39 (bc) William Manning/Corbis; (bl) Andre Jenny/Alamy; 40 (b) Angela Hampton Picture Library/Alamy; 41 (b) Bill Freeman / PhotoEdit; (t) Tina Minale/Alamy; 44 (b) Tannen Maury/The Image Works Image; 45 (tr) Bettmann/Corbis; (br) Corbis SYGMA; (cr) Oliver Maire/Keystone/Corbis; 46 (b) Park Street / PhotoEdit; 56 (b) Tina Manley/Alamy; (cr) Bettmann/Corbis; 57 (bl) AP Photo/Rich Pedroncelli; 62 (bl) Gary Vestal/ Getty Images; 63 (cl) Comstock Images/Getty Images; (cr) Tony Fagan/Alamy; (br) Joe McDonald/Corbis; 66 (b) Juniors Bildarchiv/photolibrary; 69 (t) Leszczynski, Zigmund / Animals Animals - Earth Scenes; 70 (b) Mike Dobel / Alamy; 72 (t) Martin Harvey/Getty Images; 72 (br) Alistair Berg/Digital Vision/Getty Images; 73 (b) AP Photo/J. Carter; 77 (b) Artville/ Getty Images

All other photos are property of Houghton Mifflin Harcourt.